I0487592

Real Estate for Real People:

A Guide to Achieving Profitability in Residential Real Estate Investing

If investing in real estate is even a figment of your imagination, allow me to enlighten you before you spend one red cent.

ANTHONY VON MICKLE

iUniverse, Inc.
New York Bloomington

Real Estate For Real People
A Guide to Achieving Profitability in Residential Real Estate Investing

iUniverse books may be ordered through booksellers or by contacting:

iUniverse
1663 Liberty Drive
Bloomington, IN 47403
www.iuniverse.com
1-800-Authors (1-800-288-4677)

ISBN: 978-0-595-47555-1 (pbk)
ISBN: 978-0-595-71160-4 (cloth)
ISBN: 978-0-595-91824-9 (ebk)

Printed in the United States of America

Contents

Acknowledgments

I would like to thank God for the opportunity to have both good investing seasons and bad ones. Without experiencing a dismal season after a very prosperous one, this book would have never been written. If every day was a great day in investing, I would never truly know how well I was doing. It is during the trials that I realized when I was taking the wrong steps. Any man can hold the helm when the sea is calm, but it was when the storms of life were raging that I truly determined what I was made of.

Special thanks go out to Mike Jenkins, Chris Collins, and Charlie Dean for planting the seed for The Investment Forum in September 2004 while sitting on overhead at Headstrong Consulting, waiting for our assignments to go to the client's site. Without you all, who knows if The Investment Forum would have ever been founded? I would also like to thank the people who have supported The Investment Forum from its very first forum, held on January 15, 2005, until now. Thanks to the Mickle family, especially John, chief strategist, and Annie, director of operations, for supporting the endeavor.

I have to give an even bigger thanks to Lamar Hough for calling me early on July 3, 2007, to share with me the good news that he bought his first investment property. It was then that I began to alert him of all the things he might encounter along the way. That conversation was what sparked the idea of writing this book. Lamar has been a lifelong friend and a brother, and I certainly did not want to see him make the mistakes I made. Thanks a million, my friend!

Another huge thank-you goes out to Carol Meininger for creating Model Home Temps Inc. (MHT). Thanks also to everyone at MHT for calling me at all those eleventh hours—especially you, Van. Thanks, Nicole, for bugging the heck out of me to take the job in the first place.

I'd like to thank Pam McGregor, Lisa Kennedy, Fran McGee, Darrell Shields, Sharon Jackson, and all the other senior management and members of BAE Systems Government Consulting Group. To anyone I overlooked, please know that I gain something that goes into my projects from everyone I meet. So if I left your name off, please forgive me, and know that you contributed to my success in one form or another. With all that being said, enjoy your investing journey.

**Something to think about

Periodically, you will find these notes to indicate important things to watch out for.

A Note to the Reader

Thank you for choosing *A Guide to Achieving Profitability in Residential Real Estate Investing* from The Investment Forum, LLC. I understand that you could have chosen any number of sources for your investing education and real estate experience, but you decided to give this book a try. I am sure you will find it helpful throughout your investment experience. Many people move too fast, but remember that there is no hurry in this business, and arming yourself with the right people and the right opportunities can provide you with significant monetary reward.

Do not confine yourself to just one source for your investment education. You should build a library of books, magazines, and other sources over the years that you can refer to from time to time. I have provided a short list of such useful resources at the end of this book, but even that is just a start. I recommend that you refer to this book each time you look to make a real estate investment so you will begin to train yourself not to overlook pertinent details.

I have seen quite a few infomercials that make real estate investing seem like a cinch. Always remember, nothing that lucrative is easy, or everybody would be rich. Do not think that this is child's play or you will quickly be thrown back into the reality of adulthood. Just like a marriage, real estate requires work. But after you get up and running and observe a full real estate business cycle with both the ups and downs, you will find it quite manageable.

How to use this book:

Although this book contains several examples of real estate experiences, it is designed as a guide. You can check the table of contents when looking for information at various stages of your investment process. The chapters are short for quick reading. It is written for long-term investors or those who are not into flipping properties. Flipping occurs when you purchase a property and look to sell it quickly at a profit. Sometimes flippers purchase the homes, fix them up, and then sell them at handsome profits; but again, that is not the intent of this book. A number of books talk about making money in foreclosures, which is also a lucrative market. While some of the basic investing principles may be the same as those listed here, making money in foreclosures is not necessarily the intent of this book, either.

I've have attempted to put these chapters in an order that you can follow chronologically so you will be able to refer to them at any point along your investment process. I understand that some deals will come to you from people who, for instance, feel they have ensured that the property is in the right community or has been well researched, but you should become familiar with taking due diligence and with the process of how to choose great properties regardless of special situations when you are introduced to a deal part way through the process.

For your added benefit, I encourage you to check out The Investment Forum's Web site for updated information about a number of investment topics, which can be found at www.vonzforum.com.

Again, thank you for choosing *Real Estate for Real People*. Please look for my future guides on equity investments and other business opportunities. Enjoy the book, be safe in your investments, make some money, and have some fun!

Anthony "Von" Mickle
The Investment Forum, president

The Von Mickle/MHT Story

I was born in Cassatt, South Carolina, as the middle child between two brothers, Trent and Willie Jr. My parents Willie and Dorothy were good parents and fairly well-known throughout our community. There really wasn't much to do if you were seeking an exciting career in our beloved Kershaw County. We were just regular people. For years I had no idea we were so economically disadvantaged. I probably didn't know because everyone I knew was pretty much in the same boat.

One thing I did recall about our community was the cohesiveness. We had a store that was founded by my aunt, who we called Bo-Peep. To this day I have no idea where that name came from. Everyone in or around our community knew that store as Bobby Brown's (which was the name of my uncle)—and no, not that notorious guy from the R&B group New Edition. Brown's was a place where the entire community would hang out, and rather frequently.

Brown's was everything our community wanted. It was divided into three areas. The area to the far left was a liquor store for the adults—but mostly just for the men. If you purchased some unknown quantity of liquor, Brown would cash your check for you. That was certainly great for him, because after the men cashed their checks, they generally gave the money back to him by buying more liquor.

The middle portion of the store was much more family oriented. There was a grill where Bo-Peep would sell hamburgers and hot dogs. Parents would sit at the bar and socialize with their friends, while kids would take advantage of the pinball and Pac-Man machines. There was also a jukebox that played our favorite songs.

The section off to the right was a dance hall. Every Thursday through Sunday the adults would party to the sounds of WPBP (Washington Park's Black Prince). He was the best DJ in town and that was his territory. When the adults weren't paying attention, us kids would sneak in there to practice dance moves we'd learned.

This store had to be a part of the village that Hillary Clinton talks about in *It Takes a Village*. If you lived in our area, you were raised by the entire village. It was commonplace to get a little firm talking-to, and maybe even a bottom warming, from any adult in the community if you deserved it. God forbid you misbehaved and it got back to your parents. That generally meant double trouble.

For the most part, I was a regular kid who lived in the trailer park and had dreams of one day living in a really nice home. I listened a bit more to my family, teachers, and community leaders than most kids and thought that I was a bit more likely to make it. When I was growing up in the '70s, South Carolina was still dominated by the ideas of Jim Crow laws, which meant that everything was fine as long as black people stayed on their side of town and white people stayed on theirs. Even then I could see that my parents wanted higher-paying jobs and the opportunity to live in a more economically stable environment, but the good ole boy mentality prevailed.

I was mostly quiet until I got to high school. We moved from a much older mobile home to a brand new one as I transitioned from the eighth grade at Camden Middle School to North Central High School. It was amazing what a new house did for my confidence. All of a sudden I thought I could now join the elite crowd and not have to shy away to the back of the room. I began to really excel at many things, and I declare it was due to my newfound confidence as the resident of a brand-new mobile home that cost all of eighteen thousand dollars in 1986.

While in high school, I joined the JROTC and was sure I was going to go into the military for at least twenty years. The JROTC program added gasoline to my newly lit confidence fire. A lot of that had to do with Lieutenant Colonel Robert McKenzie and Command

Sergeant Major Teddy Osborne, two of the finest instructors that were ever born. They had been around young adults for so long that they knew how to push and motivate us. They were involved in our lives like parents, and sometimes even more so. They introduced so many of us to a world outside of the small county we grew up in. I quickly became a standout and was rapidly promoted to prove it. I had a level of confidence that made me feel like I was capable of doing anything I wanted to do. After that experience, I knew that the army was surely where my career would begin.

When it was time to consider life after high school, I decided to attend The Citadel, The Military College of South Carolina. In fact, Command Sergeant Major Osborne drove me two hours to the college for my weekend visit. I spent my next four years studying French and business while wearing a uniform in an all-male environment. Not having any women around wasn't particularly fun at first, but I adjusted. When the first woman attended the school, I welcomed her, but I was one out of two thousand. That decision made me both extremely popular and unwelcome at the same time.

I fulfilled my academic requirements but decided I would not go full-time into the military. During knob (freshman) year, I made an eight-year commitment to the Army National Guard. Since I was not on active duty and did not have a full-time obligation, I could go to graduate school wherever I wanted. For whatever reason, I was curious about foreign languages at the time and decided to continue my language studies at Harvard University's Ukrainian research program.

For me, Harvard was an interesting place to be. I didn't feel that my trailer park background fit in any more there than it had at The Citadel. These were purely economic issues; in class, I was treated the same as anyone else. It did not matter why a young black guy from a rural trailer park would want to attend The Citadel to study French any more than it mattered why he'd want to attend Harvard to study Ukrainian.

After my stint in Cambridge, Massachusetts, I moved to the Washington DC metro area in May of 1997 in search of a job. I wanted to get into the information technology (IT) field, which was thriving at the time. Many young professionals were earning good salaries with little experience. It was also a successful career choice because of the influx of government jobs that required security clearances at various levels.

My aunt Annie was stationed at Fort Belvoir in Alexandria, Virginia. She allowed me to stay with her rent free for a full year before sending me to the streets. She provided me with a lot of exposure on everything from the military to fitness to the power of home ownership. Actually, she *dwelled* on home ownership. I knew one day I wanted to live in a really big, nice house but really did not know when that day would come. I accompanied her on many trips to view townhouses, condos, and single-family homes, as we were always out looking. Although I paid some attention to the home shopping she was doing, I was really more interested in getting an information technology job.

I began my technical career as a contractor for GTE (currently Verizon) as a help-desk technician. I was sure that I wanted to become a database developer for no other reason than it sounded like a fancy title, and because I heard that they were making nearly eighty thousand dollars annually with a degree and a few years of experience. But I soon realized that this was not the track that I wanted to be on and began to make progress on the network engineering division of GTE. Over the next several years, I took several successive jobs involving networks and soon found myself working for British Telecom (BT) as a technical manager. Since I was making headway and a solid name for myself among the senior managers, I was sure that I would be on track to reach my ultimate goal as CEO.

At the turn of the century, many of the technical companies began to feel the woes of the Y2K compliance problem. British Telecom made it successfully into the year 2000 without the life-ending computer meltdown everyone expected, but it soon began to experience many other business issues. I moved from BT to Concert, a joint venture between BT and AT&T. Around that time, telecom companies were buying office space and Cisco network engineering equipment by the pound, thinking that the need for further growth would continue for a lot longer than they anticipated.

Little did they—or I—know that their services would no longer be needed. In April of 2001, I received a summons to the VP's office to find out that I was being laid off. I thought surely this was nuts, as I had only worked for four years and layoffs only happened to seasoned people. Since I was young and degreed while working on an MBA, I had assumed I was safe. At the very least, I assumed that I'd be back to work in another telecom or similar job within a few days or weeks.

The economy was about to take a major change. The dot-coms turned into "dot-bombs," and we were quickly met by the attacks of September 11, 2001. After that, it seemed the only way to get any government or technical work was by having a top-secret clearance. Clearances were essentially background checks that were initiated to ensure you were who you said you were. They were issued by government agencies or the companies that supported those agencies. It took up to twelve months, at the time, for a thorough investigation, and the list to get one was a mile long. All of these things coupled together made for a very difficult economic year for quite a number of people.

One of the things that really carried me during this time was the fact that I had listened to my aunt. Instead of renting an apartment, I used my benefits gained from my time serving as an infantryman in the South Carolina Army National Guard to purchase my first house with no money down. That was worth its weight in platinum for the benefit it would provide over the next several years.

During the eighteen months I was out of work, I continued to diligently search for new technical roles. Unfortunately, I was not finding any suitable opportunities regardless of what I tried. Several of my colleagues had also been laid off and were having a tough time getting back into well-paying jobs. One close friend of mine, Nicole Black, turned to a local paper to find a job working as an assistant to homes sales managers for a company called Model Home Temps Inc. (MHT).

MHT was founded by a former real estate agent who realized that there was a need for the help of a lightly trained assistant when the sales manager was writing a contract for a home buyer. When buying a home, the paperwork can be tedious and in some cases can take hours to complete. Meanwhile, other visiting customers are still in need of sales assistance with questions regarding the community, options, floor plans, and so on. In these instances, a temporary assistant works out very well, as they can answer a lot of the basic questions. Many builders have assistants on hand, but if the assistant has an emergency, then a temporary aide is still needed.

Nicole took the MHT assignment and was really enjoying her time, but she was only being compensated twelve dollars per hour. I initially thought she was not making the best use of her time by taking that job, as she had been making one hundred dollars an hour before her IT contract ended. She appeared content, however, and before long was working side-by-side with the business owner to call on some of the many employees for assignments.

One day in July of 2001, Nicole asked me if I would be interested in going out to a model home. I couldn't believe she was even asking me. I felt my time was better spent trying to get another full-time, salaried IT assignment. She was diligent about it, and I perpetually told her no. I figured if she wasn't smart enough to realize her time could be better spent looking for another technical role, then surely I wasn't going to join her.

But her persistence paid off, and after multiple calls, I eventually broke down and gave showing homes a try. Since I didn't have a government clearance, it was not like I was busy going on interviews. I reluctantly went to the home of the business owner of MHT Inc. for my initial training alongside another gentleman who signed up. We spent a few afternoon hours listening to the dos and don'ts of MHT. Before long I was off to my first site and was trained by a middle-aged woman named Wanda in a townhouse in Dumfries, Virginia. As I sat there in the newly built townhome, I began to reflect on my own three-year-old townhome and thought, this one is slightly bigger than mine, but at $168,000, it also costs $60,000 more. As I sat there I started to recognize how nice the place was. Everything was brand new and had that nice, new-home smell. I quickly found that once you are in a new model home by yourself, you begin to take ownership and think, "If only this were mine."

When visitors came into the home, as long as I presented myself like a professional, many of them respected me as if I was the builder himself—or at the very least like I was the most knowledgeable sales manager they had ever met. It certainly helped that instead of renting an apartment I had bought my own house, as my aunt had instructed. Because I had a similar home to the ones I was showing, I could reflect on my experiences as a homeowner and was able to share some knowledge with many other potential first-time homeowners. The respect the visitors gave me felt very rewarding. It was an introduction that let me know that I had more knowledge of home ownership than I gave myself credit for. Before this experience, I had simply figured everyone else had the same knowledge.

I rather enjoyed the experience, even though it only paid eight dollars per hour. I knew I wasn't missing much, other than another job fair at which employers would say I could work only if I had a top secret clearance. MHT asked if I could come back the next day, and I did. Several days went by, and they called again to see if I could go to another townhouse. I quickly became a standout among my peers. After visiting a few townhomes, I started thinking how I would really like to work in a single-family home. Single-family homes are generally bigger and allow the buyer more options than a townhouse offers.

I had been curious about the affordability of single-family homes, as my home was $108,000 with a $900-a-month mortgage payment. I noticed that many single-family homes at that time came with price tags of at least $300,000. I wondered how in the world people could afford that. I thought they would have had payments of $2,700 a month, and I surely did not know anyone who could shell out that kind of cash for a mortgage. Because I was still relatively new to the workforce, I was thinking a salary of $80,000 annually was pretty strong and didn't personally know a lot of people who made much more than that. It wasn't long before I got my chance to work in a single-family home, and I was so impressed by this model that I felt that it was the type of home I deserved to live in.

**Something to think about

If you find something that you really, really want, I recommend that you take a picture of it! I have found that by doing this you are telling yourself consciously that this is something you desire. When you take a picture of it, it becomes a part of you, and your mind will not let you forget it until this thing that you desire becomes yours in reality.

Several years ago while I was in high school, I came across a house that I really liked in an area of Columbia, South Carolina, known as Wild Wood. This was a golf-course community filled with nice houses. One house in particular somehow grabbed my attention substantially more than the others. Before seeing this house, I had never seen stucco siding and didn't know what it was, but I really liked it. This particular home was gold and had a two-car, side-load garage. It was neat the way the house was turned sideways, showing the length of its side more so than the length of the front from the street, like the more traditional houses.

One day I decided to take a picture of the house. I had no plans for the picture other than the thought that one day I would like to build something similar. I didn't look at the picture regularly. I never wrote any goals down about building the house. I simply knew that I really, really liked that house, so I took a picture of it.

When I got involved in real estate investing years later and decided I wanted to move into a single-family house, I found a community that reminded me of my days at The Citadel and life in Charleston, South Carolina. Much like the house I saw in Wild Wood years earlier, these homes were turned to display their sides to the street. To purchase such a home, I rented out my townhome and wrote the contract on the new home through a cash-out refinance (discussed in The Power of Home

Equity chapter. As I was writing the contract, I told the sales manager of the similarity between the community here in Manassas, Virginia, and the homes in Charleston. She smiled and said, "Well, I guess it worked, because that's exactly what we were trying to do."

The model I chose was called the Hallard. The homes came with several siding options, which included Hardiplank siding, brick, and stucco. For those who chose stucco, there were three colors to chose from, one of which one was gold. The Hallard model was a very unique and stylish floor plan, as it was designed with a two-car, side-load garage. I was excited about my chance to build my very first single-family home in an upscale neighborhood and couldn't wait to begin construction.

However, I knew there was something very serendipitous about this purchase. There was something more going on that I couldn't quite place my finger on until several weeks later. As I drove to South Carolina to show my parents the blueprints, I thought about the home in Wild Wood that I had dreamed about and had taken a picture of. Without even so much as writing a plan for building that house, the plan magically came to fruition.

When I figured out what had happened, I was completely overwhelmed. Instead of going directly to my parents' house, I decided to drive back to Wild Wood. Wouldn't you know it, the same house that motivated me to take a picture turned out to pale in size compared to the home I was building.

As much as some may initially think that this was a coincidence, I have to tell you that taking pictures of the things I wanted and having them magically appear in my life has happened many, many times. I have experienced this with furniture, jewelry, cars, and even my own physique. After I witnessed this several times, I realized it wasn't magic at all. When you take a picture of something you desire, I believe you burn a mental image into your subconscious mind, and whether you actively pursue it or not, your brain continues to look for the image you've given it. Regardless of whether you provide a roadmap to whatever it is, your subconscious will not stop working until it finds what you have programmed it to reach for. The only way your mind stops seeking what you have shown it is if you provide it with either what you have requested or something even greater. I've heard some call it the law of attraction. I have come to believe that you can speak things into existence, whether they are good or bad. With that being said, it is very important that you focus on positive things, because if you provide your mind with negative mental images, it will give you exactly what you have fed it.

While I don't recommend that you aimlessly go out taking pictures of everything you see, the things that just "do it" for you are worth your time to place in the lens of a camera.

I currently reside in a 7,500-square-foot estate home. While I was absolutely certain that it would be out of my price range for many years, I decided to take a picture of a magnificent two-acre estate home anyway. It wasn't one full year later that I was writing the contract on my home, which happened to be on ten acres. I have been told that coincidences are God's way of remaining anonymous. I think God will reward you with what you desire if you truly desire it and are willing to work for it. Some people call this faith. The picture is substance of the thing that is hoped for and the evidence of the thing now seen.

I thought taking pictures was a silly little idea that only I had and kept to myself, but I found out via a Mary Kay representative who visited my home and noticed a large picture of my dream house on the wall that this was actually a strategy of motivational thinking for highly successful people. I have mentioned this concept during my investment forums, and a young lady named Laurie once asked me something that I had never been asked before. She said, "Have you ever taken a picture of something that you didn't get?" I thought about it for a moment and said, "No, actually, I haven't." Now, I will admit that while the estate home I built wasn't exactly like the one in the picture, it isn't very far from it.

One day while I was working for MHT, one of the home buyers called in and requested that I go through their file to check on some information that was submitted. As I flipped through, I couldn't help noticing that the couple made $70,000 a year combined and had more financial obligations than I had. It was then that I began to realize that mortgage companies would give out loans on real estate with qualifications less stringent than I assumed. For some reason, I was under the impression that if you were going to be given a loan of more than $300,000, then surely you would need to earn $150,000 annually. I could not have been more wrong.

Over the next several weeks I continued to work at a number of different models, many of them single-family homes. I began to realize that customers called in all the time to request information that was in their files, which invariably gave me the opportunity to see what was required financially to make purchases of various types of homes. I was very surprised many times to find that the money I thought was needed to buy a certain house was not even close to what was actually required to get a loan and make the purchase. This is not to say banks and other lenders did not do a good job of qualifying home buyers. Instead, it just illustrates my then-uneducated interpretation of what was required to buy in the local market.

As my confidence and skill set in this new field grew, MHT's confidence level in me grew, and they began to send me to some of the more exclusive communities. Homes there generally cost more than $500,000, and the buyers typically were not first-time homeowners. These buyers required more specialized assistance. As I began going to more and more of these sites, I became more knowledgeable about what it took to own these higher-end homes and also became more curious about what buyers needed to bring to the closing table. I had many conversations with the sales managers about what was required to purchase. Most of them were willing to provide the information I was looking for. After all, they knew that I would some day be going back to my field of information technology and was highly likely to return as a buyer. I continued to visit more and more sites and thought of more and more questions. In addition, I kept plenty of film in my camera, and I took a lot of pictures of these lovely homes.

Before I knew it, eighteen months had passed by, and I was finally getting set to go back to work full-time as an IT professional. It had been a long and trying time because my income had been cut substantially. I decided that the knowledge I gained was so valuable to my future that when I got back into a full-time job, I would continue working with MHT on the weekends. By this time I had become quite a fan of luxury homes, as they gave me a chance to see what I called the American Dream of homeownership. For many years before having the MHT job, I had observed beautiful homes with awe and guessed what they must look like inside. I had never had the opportunity to visit anyone with a luxury home before then.

I was playing a game of pool one July evening in 1999 with some friends, and I told Rex, a BT colleague, about how I admired lovely homes. He recommended that I take a drive through Potomac, Maryland, and said I'd probably find exactly what I was looking for in that town. I had observed the exit to Potomac many times as I drove around the Beltway, but because I didn't know anyone out there, I had never ventured into the area. After chatting with Rex, I decided to make a visit. When I turned off at the River Road exit, it wasn't very long before I realized I had found precisely what I was looking for. The homes screamed elegance and wealth.

As I perused the main road and side streets, I was absolutely awestruck. I had never experienced this type of community and could only think that surely this is the lifestyle of the rich and famous. These mammoth abodes had everything the eye could imagine that the brain hadn't begun to conceive. And there was one right after the other.

Not only were the homes beautiful and over the top, but so were the automobiles. I had heard many times that a person can live in a nice house if he or she decides to drive less expensive cars. These homes had an appearance of wealth, and their cars went right along with the image. They showcased Ferraris, Bentleys, Mercedes, BMWs, and more. In many cases, homeowners seemed to have one of each. The garages should have been called bays and were more like exotic, European showrooms. I was told that I would find Washington's elite class in this neighborhood, and if I were an equestrian or scratch golfer, this was the place to be. Tiger Woods had played in major golf tournaments in this very community.

I later found that many of these homes were built by Niroo Construction, Inc. The company is ran by David and Haleh Niroo who have made an exceptional name for themselves in the area. In 2008, the Travel Channel featured the company on an episode of their "Great Taste" series. David presides over the company and the construction while his lovely wife Haleh, who is also regarded as one of the area's most extraordinary interior designers, takes care of the design. Together they have enhanced the landscape of Washington Metro area suburbs.

I decided to accept what I was seeing at face value and tried not to read too much into it. Some people, and perhaps rightfully so, may feel that communities like these are filled with people who live wildly beyond their means and are up to their necks in debt. Some people would prefer to be "the millionaire next door," but I didn't want entertain that thought. I accepted what I saw because it was very motivating for me. Since I was going back to work full-time, I would not get an opportunity to work in such a neighborhood during the week. But I wanted MHT to keep me in mind when they received a call for help from this community.

I drove through Potomac many more times on my own to dream. While MHT mentioned they sent people to this area, many of the homes were custom built and did not require a model. It only made sense—it seemed these mansions were just as varied as they were big. One day I finally got my opportunity, as one of the builders needed a temporary aide for the weekend and MHT called me, knowing I was more than interested.

When I arrived, I was a bit disappointed. I thought I'd find some beautiful mansion awaiting me. Instead I found that no homes were constructed yet, and the sales manager was working out of a trailer. Trailers were more common than I knew before getting into the model home world, and I had my own idea about how they might look inside. However, these trailers were much different from what I grew up in or some motion picture's attempt to display the home of less fortunate people. In fact, I recall seeing a show on million-dollar mobile home communities. That show let me know that trailers were more than just homes for people who either could not or would not spend money for a single-family home.

Trailers were used in place of a nicely decorated model while the builders cleared off land to begin construction. These single-wide trailers had class. They had to. You have to figure that if you are about to sell someone a home with a price tag of half a million dollars and the sellers have to go into a trailer to write the contract, the trailer has to be very nice. I had to give the builders credit for the way they set up these temporary—yet contemporary—sales offices. They were filled with large, full-color displays of what a new home would look like, with additional full-color displays dedicated to some of the more popular options that a homeowner might select.

I entered the temporary sales site, greeted the manager as normal, and asked her what I might do to help her out that weekend. She probably assumed me to be just another temp sent out to help make brochures for the day. She pointed me to the phones and instructed me on what types of calls I would most likely receive. Meanwhile, she was preparing to change clothes to show potential customers how their homes might be constructed on the muddy, unexcavated land. Because of the price range and the remote location, things were a bit slow at first in terms of phone calls and customer visits. In the early going, I didn't come across any information that would give me a better idea of what types of people were able to buy such extravagant houses.

Several hours later, I finally got what I was looking for. Someone called in to ask about a home they had purchased and needed me to look through their file for a floor covering color. I gladly opened the file and gave the information that the customer requested. It was then that I found something that changed my residential life.

The file belonged to a middle-aged man who was purchasing a home for $1,000,000. Although I found a purchase of that price to be quite an accomplishment, it wasn't nearly as surprising as what I was about to see next. As I flipped through the file to find his requested information, I could not help noticing his qualifying numbers. He had an income of only $55,000 a year! I thought, how in the world can anyone afford a million-dollar home when all they make is fifty-five grand?

I looked closely at the file and noticed that he had five bank accounts. Each account had a balance ranging from $15,000 to $45,000. At that point I was under the impression that he had a lot of money. Then I thought about it and figured that this money would soon run out based on the $900,000 mortgage and assuming he put 10 percent down. His monthly income before taxes would not begin to cover this amount. I looked a bit closer and realized that he also had four other homes. Each home was being rented out, so he was apparently making his mortgage payments, but he couldn't have made much beyond that. The rental income his other properties generated wasn't going to be enough to add any substantial equity money to his new home.

After spending a few minutes browsing the documents, I realized that the money sitting in those bank accounts was all borrowed money. These were home equity loans or home equity lines of credit. He looked very good on paper because he was using OPM ("other people's money"). Then something grabbed me even more. The statements listed all of the mortgages that he had and the loan amounts. One loan in particular held my attention because it was similar to the loan on my new home. His loan balance was $460,000. His payment was $1,400 a month, while my payment was $2,650 on a $463,000 loan. Instantly I thought, how could his payment be substantially less than mine when I have a 5 percent interest rate? My credit was good, and 5 percent was about the best rate I saw advertised when I bought the house. I pulled out my calculator and figured that his loan payment had to be only 1 percent. I had never heard of such a loan and wondered how he could have gotten it.

Soon afterward I called the bank, and they told me that yes, I could, in fact, get a loan at a 1 percent interest rate. The loan was called the Option ARM. I wondered why I had never heard of this before and figured that none of my friends had heard of it, either. I started to diligently research what was required to obtain that kind of loan while telling all of my friends what I had discovered. I called together a meeting of my friends to discuss this.

**Something to think about
Be sure to research all loans fully and ensure that you understand all phases of them before you agree to terms.

Please note that I did not charge full speed ahead into this loan! I researched diligently to find out as much as I could about the product. Not all loans are meant for everyone, and the Option ARM loan certainly fits that bill. I simply looked for knowledge of what was out there concerning this type of loan. I am in no way recommending anyone take on a mortgage that they should not have.

Option ARM loans work well for some people with varying incomes, such as sales professionals, who are subject to receive little money during part of the year but substantially more later in the year. This allows them to make a minimum payment during the slow times with the intention of making a much higher payment later. It is called Option ARM because it gives the loan holder a choice of making a minimum payment, an interest-only payment, payments based on fifteen-year fixed rates, or payments based on thirty-year fixed rates. The consumer has the option to choose the best terms for them each month.

I believe that many people are not exposed to and aware of the same types of investments that others are. In some cases, this is for good reason, as investments are not designed for everyone. However, exposure is still essential. You never know when your situation may change, so if you have at least been exposed to different types of investment vehicles, you can take advantage of the right ones when the time is right. I believe that such lack of knowledge keeps some people from playing the game on even terms, and it certainly prevents some people from ever obtaining the things they dream of. When you have exposure to more information, you are playing on more even terms with other investors. That is why I called together that meeting of my friends to discuss the Option ARM loan. I set a theme for the meeting: "The Uneven Playing Field." Today, that meeting group is called The Investment Forum.

But still, why should you listen to me?

Once The Investment Forum got underway, I became its most eager student. Not only did I listen to others, but I also listened to myself. I begin to tap into the power of home equity. I also began reading lots of books. I read *Rich Dad, Poor Dad* by Robert Kiyosaki. I also read Donald Trump's *Think Like a Billionaire.* I would venture to say that reading Donald Trump's book had one of the biggest impacts on my life for the next two years, all for one reason.

Trump mentions that you absolutely have to read! I have to admit that while I was a strong believer in education and had an MBA, I was only used to reading textbooks. The last thing I wanted to do was read for "fun." I wasn't the least bit interested in romance novels and steamy love stories, but I was being quite stupid. While wondering how the rich people were so well off, I was avoiding the obvious—they got rich by reading. When you read the stories of how the rich made their fortunes, they give you insight and details on what challenges they faced and how they overcame those challenges. When I realized the great stories that could be found in books on how people became successful, it became very entertaining to me and educational at the same time. For this reason I encourage everyone to read as much as possible. Please refer to the Suggested Additional Reading section located near the end of the book for a list of books I've found most useful.

After I finished reading Trump's book, I was hooked like a kid on a new game system. I was absolutely overwhelmed by the insight that books like his provided. They were illustrating their authors' thought processes on life and business. As I implemented these ideas, my net worth rapidly increased. Before I could blink I went from having $150,000 worth of investments to just over $3,000,000. It all came about simply because I changed my way of thinking by adapting the thinking of the wealthy. I found that the wealthy had four common principles that would always allow them to overcome financial pitfalls, so I developed an acronym that I call "PTFL," pronounced "pitfall." The acronym stands for passion, timing, fear, and leverage.

Passion, to me, means doing what you love to do whether you get paid to do it or pay to do it. In nearly every book I read about wealthy people, I read that each of them was passionate about what they did. In fact, these people all knew that if you don't love what you do, you may as well quit, because your odds of becoming wealthy from it are slim to none. When you love what you do, you do not have to force yourself to keep doing it. In fact, you do not even consider it work.

Once you fully engage yourself into whatever it is that makes you happy, people around you begin to notice because you probably talk about your passion more than they want to hear about it. That alone lets them know where your interests are. They can hear the intensity in your voice and see the passion in your movements.

Passion is very contagious when it is set free in an environment that welcomes it. When you are passionate about what you are doing, people around you become stakeholders in your endeavors, and they start to tell other people about you the second they hear a similar conversation or see similar interests to what you've been telling them about. This type of fire creates a domino effect and allows someone who is not even a natural networker to be placed in the company of the best and brightest just by following his or her heart.

You do not have to waste your time in the company of successful people trying to make small talk and telling them how you are their biggest fan in an attempt to catch some secret to success. Wealthy and highly successful people know who's who and can spot a phony a mile away. They can tell who is passionate about what they do.

Timing is not something that wealthy people have on their side just by chance. They all understand that the perfect time to invest never comes. They realize that the time is now. You can read all the books from all the greatest authors, but if you never take the time to act on the principles, you are just another educated soul suffering from paralysis by analysis. Some investments will be made when the time is just right, but the chance of making them all at the perfect time is zero.

After people have made investments and mistakes, they learn from their mistakes, and the next time, they make better decisions. Before long, they are well ahead of the game, and it seems that every decision they make happened at the perfect time. But what people are actually seeing is instance after instance of those people getting a little better at what they do each time they do it.

Fear is something that wealthy people have but they do not allow it to consume them. They recognize it as a feeling that can be overcome by time and experience. For example, one evening in 2003, I was on Capitol Hill at an event sponsored by The Citadel where we welcomed all the newly elected officials from South Carolina. I was having a conversation with one of our distinguished alumni, Congressman Steve Buyer. We were talking about a job that I had recently interviewed for with Goldman Sachs. I told him they were looking for a group of people to work with their high-net-worth clients, or those who had a minimum of $3,000,000 in assets. I told him I was shocked that there was an entire market of people around Washington who fit that category.

He quickly interrupted, "Oh, more than that!" I told him I didn't get it. I was feeling good about having a six-figure salary and living in a very nice neighborhood, but I knew I didn't even come close to matching the wealth of some of the guys I read about in the newspapers, like Michael Dell or some of the other filthy-rich guys. I asked him what in the world the difference was between me and guys like that.

He replied, "They have no fear." He went on to say it was funny that I mentioned Dell, because just the night prior he had had dinner with a CXO of Dell Computers and a few CEOs of other large U.S. companies. He said, "It is amazing to see how they think. They have made hundreds of millions and they are ready to put it all on the line." Still a bit puzzled, I asked him how, and he began to explain the next letter of the acronym.

Leverage is using some of what you already have to obtain something greater. Congressman Buyer said, "They will risk it all and bet the whole farm, and not only that, they will do it today." That is how it is done. You have to be willing to leverage some of what you have to gain something more.

Leverage is probably the most executable word in the PTFL acronym. It has certainly been the one that has led me to the enormous amount of financial growth I've experienced. When I stopped being scared to be passionate about what I liked doing and understood that leveraging my current assets would be the way to wealth, rather than the much-appreciated, yet slow-growing "savings" strategy, my asset column grew tremendously. Let's face it—I'm not going to drive a Lamborghini Murcielago because I diligently put $100 a month into my savings account, but leveraging the equity of one property to buy another one and profit tens and thousands of dollars in the process makes the $400,000 supercar a very reachable reality.

Years ago, I came up with a question: "If you're always hanging around people who aren't going anywhere, where in the hell do you think you're going?" I then instituted my *big* philosophy:

If you think big, you act big.
If you act big, you look big.
If you look big, you feel big.
If you feel big, you are big.

Once you feel big in your heart and mind, there is no stopping your success. You simply have to rid yourself of the naysayers and people who are stuck thinking small and wonder why they can't get where they want to go.

You may wonder why I would write a book about the information that successful people often keep to themselves, even though I am deep in admiration of those people. It is not so much that I am writing against them, but I have learned from being their student, and my own experience is that they are so successful that some of the very critical pitfalls that can lead to failure have been left out of their works. Since I have a ways to go before I'm truly successful, I feel that I am more closely connected to the guy who is just starting out than the likes of Donald Trump or Dr. Dolf de Roos, author of *Real Estate Riches*. High-rollers like them may not have come across some of the problems mentioned in this book in years. With that in mind, let's get into the heart of the subject: how I can educate you on making money in real estate.

Getting Started
"The Essence of Survival"

Every morning in Africa, a gazelle wakes up. It knows is must run faster than the fastest lion or it will be killed. Every morning a lion wakes up. It knows it must outrun the slowest gazelle or it will starve to death. It doesn't matter whether you're a lion or a gazelle. When the sun comes up, you'd better be running.
—Author unknown

**Something to think about
Money is an element of life. We live in a material world and we need materials to live. We have all heard people say that money can't buy love or it can't buy happiness. While I do understand, I have to say that I don't know any unhappy rich people. Whether you like it or love it, having extra money makes life easier.

I don't believe life as a real estate investor is as bad as kill or be killed, eat or be eaten, but I do believe that some days you are the windshield and other days you are the bug. This statement simply means that some days are better than others, and you have to decide which side of the coin you want to be on. Regardless of which side that may be, you have to hit the ground running each day. You will face tenants and insurance, real estate, and tax agents. You must present yourself as a professional to all of them all of the time. If you don't, you may get taken. Opportunities abound, and the deal of a lifetime comes along every day. The problem is that it comes along for a lot of people. Whether or not you take advantage of the opportunity is strictly up to you. You have to be crouched in the weeds blending in with the elements, and when opportunity gets within your reach, you pounce on it like the lion pounces on the gazelle.

Investing is a subject that is thought of by many but only mastered by a few. Having sufficient income to buy the things we want or to have the peace of mind we desire to live with can be obtained by solid investments. With that being said, making money is addicting. It always has been and it always will be. Many of you will make money and have more than you can spend, while others will look for additional income just to maintain life's essentials. It is exciting when you realize an investment can provide you with money that will make your life more comfortable. You may not want money for a fancy house or car, but you may want the ability to go shopping at any time or to travel wherever and whenever you want to go. Regardless of what it is you fancy, investments can give you a lot of material things.

Real estate investors are everywhere. Some rely on foreclosures, while others rely on the timing of the market. Still others have a network of friends that they rely on for the most up-to-date insight. Real estate deals are on every corner. Publications sold on local news stands list available properties. Many Web sites market properties to specific buyers and sellers, such as active-duty military men and women who are generally in one area of the country for a specified amount of time. Many of them do not look to own and prefer renting, as the government supplements their housing allowance in many cases, so Web sites available, some of them regional, list real estate investment opportunities just for them. Some cities with universities, affectionately known as "college towns," have so many students that they can outnumber the available on-campus housing units. They will look to rent properties during the school year and, many times, during the summer as well. Regardless of where your investment desire fits in on this scale, you can rest assured that you are not the only one in that category.

I invest in more than just real estate. I invest in Wall Street and directly in other businesses. I also invest in some very key components of life—myself and other people. It is essential, especially as a real estate investor, to place yourself in the company of like-minded people and hope to be in the company of people who can teach you about investments.

Inexperienced investors may be looking for their first opportunity. Experienced investors may be looking to increase their knowledge of investments by adding to their research library. In either case, let me commend you for your courage to gain further insight by reading this book. Many people have had a real estate investment idea at some point or another. The idea has occurred for some while riding through a neighborhood and noticing for-sale signs. For others, the idea may have come from infomercials late at night that have advertised common people making lots of money with little or no work and receiving residual income in their spare time. For still others, the idea may have come up because they have seen or heard of people having success in their real estate investments. Regardless of how you've come to the decision to get involved in real estate, real estate can be a very lucrative way to invest your money.

Even if you have not invested any money in a real estate venture yet, you have already deemed yourself worthy to be involved in this business. Quite a few people plop down a lot of money without so much as reading a single article, and while a few of them will get lucky, many will lose money when they didn't have to. I have read many books on the subject, from the most popular best sellers to some that were not so well-known. I have spent hundreds of hours listening to people tell of their real estate experiences, and one thing I have found that they all have in common is that no one is willing to expose all their knowledge, even if they can. The best sellers are best sellers for a reason, and that is because they are filled with good news and excitement about making money. There is nothing inherently wrong with that. However, when you consider that such books often leave out many things that people will encounter that are critical to their success or failure, I'm not particularly sure that these books are doing the readers a big favor. Concepts are left out that can end up causing an eager investor quite a bit of uneasiness that could have been avoided.

Investors' stories and experiences often paint the rosiest of pictures. While there are many rosy pictures to be painted, some investors do not do a good job of talking about what they had to encounter to get to those successful moments. Make no mistake about it, there are tons of rewarding stories out there, and I have many of my own to share. However, my goal is to paint the most complete picture that I can. In addition, I want to introduce you to things that I could have done better that would have allowed for even greater returns and stories of more success. Because many of you work nine-to-five jobs, a lot of your income is already spoken for, and the extra money you have reserved for an investment needs to go a long way without hiccups and glitches. I assure you that you will encounter both; but again, this book looks to provide you with additional experiences you will encounter that you probably will not get from many other books or sidebar conversations.

My intent is to provide you with very practical experiences of what you can expect in your investment journey. I have decided to say "journey" because it is very important to realize that you will not get rich quick. Don't even look for get-rich-quick schemes. They are the fastest way to go broke.

While I won't say hard work is necessarily involved in real estate, very diligent work is a must. You will have to keep good records and receipts of what you do. If you are not someone who is good with keeping up with paperwork, perhaps you will want to enlist the help of a friend or spouse. Another option is allowing a property management company to do this work for you, for a fee, of course. In the beginning some investors want to believe that they can handle it all themselves, and while this may be true for some, many will find that going it alone may not be the best route.

I would strongly recommend that before you get started you look at your debt ratios. This means taking a look at your financial health to ensure that you can continue to function during any unexpected events, which, I assure you, will happen. When you get to the lending stage, banks will want to see that you are not under mounds of debt, as lots of debt makes them see you as less likely to pay them back. For a more detailed idea of how to look at your financial health, you can visit www.vonzforum.com for an example.

I hope that this book will spark your interest and pique your curiosity about a number of things that you have not considered *before* you invest any more money toward a purchase. You are preparing yourself to embark on a very worthy goal. I have put together some things that will help you. My intent is to help you keep your profits by dodging pitfalls and not making costly mistakes. Keep in mind that, while investing, sometimes not losing money can be just as important as making money.

Michael Dell has been on the Forbes 400 richest list for many years now, and he is one of the youngest to appear at the billionaire level. It's no secret that he is the founder and CEO of Dell Computer. When Dell came to the personal computer scene, personal computers were not new. Many companies had been around for years. In spite of that, Dell was able to come in and gain an incredible market share. The company is highly successful for a number of reasons.

One in particular is Dell's process. Instead of stocking computers on a shelf, the company has a just-in-time delivery system. Each computer is custom-made when it is ordered. Let's think about this for a moment. If you have hundreds of thousands of customers coming to you each month to order a new computer, how on earth can you customize and deliver them in record time? The answer is process. Just as Jiffy Lube advertises that they are the "well-oiled machine," so is Dell's computer setup. They have a process so fine-tuned that they have the ability to ship custom computers very rapidly. This means everyone—from the guy who installs the motherboards to the gal who adds the monitor to the group that assembles the speakers—is in sync with the sales representative over the phone, who is in turn in sync with the delivery service that sends the PC to your door. That is a well-oiled machine.

As you look to create additional cash flow through residual income and build your wealth over the years through real estate, you will have to have a process. The real estate investors who are successful have figured this out, and now it is simply a matter of executing another transaction, just as Dell sells another computer. Now, while most of you will not buy several thousand properties per month, it is quite likely that many of you will acquire several properties over the next several years. Whether you know it or not, real estate is a "gotcha" business. It can be very exciting, and many successes can occur rapidly after getting started. That is all the more reason to realize that you have to establish a process right from the start and get comfortable with it so that when you make transactions, they will flow effortlessly.

Whether you own one property today or fifty, chances are you are looking to acquire more. You may as well get into the groove of a good process now rather than later. Poll as many successful real estate investors as you like. I assure you that if they have been successful over time, then every one of them will tell you that they have a process.

Businesses Have Cycles

If you think the cost of education is expensive, try paying for ignorance.
—Benjamin Franklin

L et's say you decide to take the family on vacation. This year you have decided to visit sunny Florida for a trip to Walt Disney World. You have already planned the trip and packed the bags. The family can't wait to see Mickey. As a parent, you are mentally preparing yourself for the high heat and long lines. You really don't want the high costs of entertainment and thousands of tourists, but hey, nothing's too good for your family, right? Besides, all your kids talk about is their opportunity to meet all the other kids from around the world in the enormous water park.

You get to Disney World and find it to be just as vibrant as the commercials and brochures have displayed. Once at the park, you notice something you didn't expect. The lines are nowhere near as long as you anticipated. It seems as if you can enjoy the major thrill rides at least five times apiece. When you visit the water park, there is hardly anyone there for your kids to play with. As you stop and wonder why the park is so empty, suddenly it hits you. It's late October. Walt Disney World can operate just as well in October as it can in July, but there are two reasons the park is empty in October. One, all the kids are back in school; and two, the outside temperature is a lot cooler than it is in July. Splashing in the water park in October could cause the kids to catch a cold. You have set out to do a great thing, but your timing couldn't be worse.

Sony doesn't release the new PlayStation during Easter any more than roses are heavily marketed for July Fourth. Products have seasons just as businesses have cycles, and you have to know when to get in and when to get out if you are going to invest. Most important, you also have to be aware of where the business cycle is when you are getting in. Real estate is no different. We have markets that favor sellers and markets that favor buyers. You don't want to be a seller in a buyer's market any more than you want to be a buyer in a seller's market. The goal is to buy low and sell high. There is no way you can do this successfully and repeatedly without understanding where in the cycle the market is at all times. Anyone can get lucky in a hot market, but sustained success comes from knowledge, wisdom, and experience.

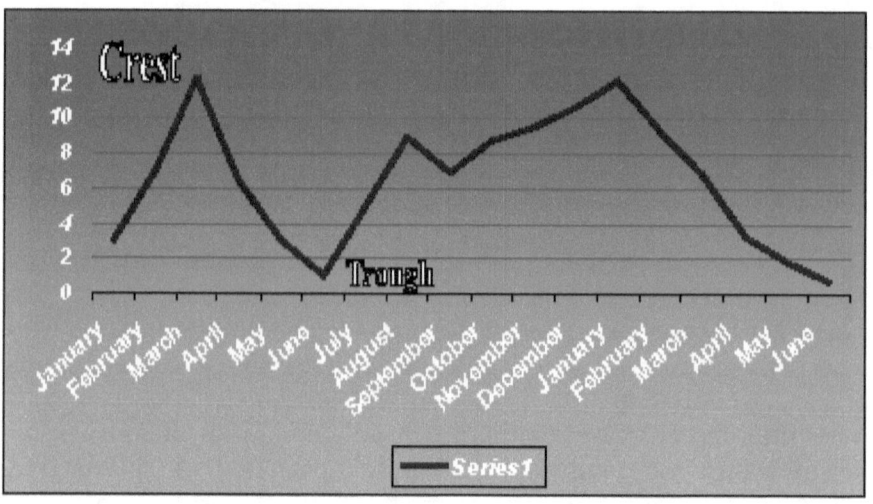

The figure above displays an eighteen-month example that shows the crests, or high points, and troughs, or low points, of a business cycle. The graph is for illustrative purposes only, as actual markets can have much longer seasons of growth or decline. The graph shows growth from January through March. In late March, we see a point where sales begin a sharp decline. The decline doesn't last long, and within a few months the market has changed and is headed back up. If you're going to make a purchase with any hopes of profiting, you certainly would not want to purchase toward the end of March with the intention of a May sale, as you would do nothing more than give away your hard-earned money.

On the other hand, if you purchase in October, you will have continued growth until January, when the market begins to cool off. Regardless of when you get into the market—and I hope you get in on the upswing—you still have to know when to get out. We'll talk more about exit strategies in another chapter, but for now it is important to understand that every market has its ups and downs.

So how do you determine when to get in? The answer is by researching the business cycle. It doesn't take an MBA to figure out where you are in the business cycle. Just ask an investor, and they will more than likely tell you. If you find that there is no one competent enough in your circle of associates to figure it out, simply watch the business news or read the business section of the newspaper. Each day, I read the *Washington Post's* business section. It is filled with information on what's going on in local business. The daily paper only costs thirty-five cents, but the benefits are worth much more.

Even having read other books and watched business infomercials, I never see any explanation of the business cycle, as they try to sell you hyperbole on making millions in your spare time. This lack of explanation to unsuspecting investors leaves many good people vulnerable to untimely market entry and exit. I strongly urge investors to take this very seriously. I invested millions in the real estate market during the upswing, but paying little attention to the business cycle made it very tough when the tides turned. This is also why you have to figure out what style of investor you are setting out to be from the beginning.

Style of investors

Many investors set out into the market without giving this subject much thought, but eventually developing your style of investment will prove to be more worthwhile than it may seem at first. One reason for this is your interaction with other investors.

If other investors see that you respond to uninformed people, they will present you with widely varying types of information—everything under the sun. They will tell you about investments that they heard of from various regions, states, and businesses, regardless of the credibility behind the investment or the person from whom they discovered it. To some investors this information overload may be okay, but what you have to realize is that if other people see that you do not do your homework first, then they will present you with opportunities that you may not actually want to pursue. In that case, you would have to waste valuable time figuring out if every single possible deal is even worthwhile in the first place.

Informed investors tend to do their homework from the start and operate with technical terms. You do not have to explain to them what equity or 1031 exchanges mean. They do not jump at the very first opportunity they see, and they will more than likely have an educated team of people that they talk with regularly to get their investment ideas. Well-informed investors generally have a much more stable and predictable track record because of this. You can generally engage in conversation with them about something that you have seen in the business or residential sections of the newspapers or about big events that are coming to town, and they will probably know what you are talking about.

Emotional investors react with their hearts. Often they will say things such as, "I have a good feeling about this," "People are going to love this," or, "No way is this going to make any money." Emotional investors tread in dangerous territory. Everyone can be lucky from time to time, but I have seen emotional investors lose a lot of money because of these personal feelings they have. There is nothing wrong with feeling good about an investment after you have done your homework, but to take a look at something and simply say you have a good or bad feeling can leave you with many days of unhappy returns.

Money is good at what it was designed for, which is spending, saving, and investing. Both having money and not having it can invoke quite a bit of emotion, but you should never put your money into something simply based on the feeling that the results might return. You may end up losing a lot of money, and that is definitely not a good feeling. On the other side of the equation, if you have a good feeling about an investment and it provides you with a great return, you may run the risk of thinking the only due diligence you need to incorporate in running your business is determining how something feels. With this mentality, sooner rather than later your feeling will prove to be wrong.

Mortgages and Asset Protection

If you owe the bank $200, you've got a problem. If you owe them
$2,000,000, they've got a problem.
—Dr. Dolf de Roos, *Real Estate Riches*

** Something to think about
At the time of this writing, the U.S. mortgage industry is taking
a bath in foreclosures due to many homeowners—and especially
investors—having received mortgages they did not understand.
With any market this is bad news for many, but good news for the
few who are have strong credit and lots of cash. As many people lose
their homes, lenders look for others who are willing to buy them. In
many cases the homes can be purchased for a fraction of their cost or
value. As an investor, you can take advantage of the troubled times,
but proceed with caution. You will still have a mortgage and need to
understand what you are getting. Even if you are in a position to buy
a property outright, you should still have a mortgage. Why should
you have a mortgage as an investor? It is better to use someone else's
money to pay for an investment than your own.

E arlier I mentioned a conversation I had with Congressman Steve
Buyer on Capitol Hill during which he described the wealth
of the CXOs he had eaten dinner with the night before. He

said the reason they were where they were was because of leverage. When it works, he said, people with great wealth and prosperity place themselves so far ahead of others that it seems impossible for anyone to fathom their wealth.

Mortgages are one of the best concepts I can use to explain leverage to investors. You have to use some of what you have and hopefully a lot of what someone else has—which is commonly called other people's money (OPM)—to get what you want. Mortgages are the key ingredient to get you to your investment. There are a ton of steps involved in mortgages, so you have to be sure that you get the right one for what you are doing. Otherwise the leverage will work against you. That means not only will your money be used against you, but so will a lot of money from someone else. For those of you who invest in equities including stocks or mutual funds, owning a mortgage is similar to trading on margin.

Before you decide on a mortgage, be sure to consult a qualified loan officer. It is even more beneficial if you can find an officer who invests and can make him or her a part of your investment team. The average person only buys a home two to three times in a lifetime, although refinances occur more frequently. Regardless, it is not every day that you sign documents like mortgage agreements. I have seen several cases where the buyer purchased a property and later came back to try and sue the lending institution. Although I do not know all the allegations, I do know that the buyers signed the loan documents, so they accepted the agreement. You don't want to find yourself in a mortgage you don't understand with your name signed on the dotted line.

I have had good and bad experiences with mortgages and the lending process. I know enough to ensure that I truly understand the type of loan I am getting before I make the purchase. Some lenders have been found guilty of predatory lending, so you always need to proceed with caution. One of the best books I've seen on mortgages is *Mortgage Confidential* by David Reed. I would recommend that you have a look at it to become well-informed about the business of mortgage loans.

As with any major purchase, you want to have your loan in hand *before* you go shopping. Surprises are lessened when you know what to expect. I would recommend letting your banking representative know what you are looking to buy in advance so they can point you toward the right loan. This goes with the concept of having a good team, which we will cover in a later chapter. In the heat of a deal, you may find that you need to move more quickly than expected, yet not hastily. When opportunities come at you fast, you may want to take the first loan coming, which may not be the best one for you.

The best way to know where you stand in terms of getting a mortgage is by knowing your FICO score. FICO scores are your report cards to the lending industry. Scores can range anywhere from 300 to 850, with the higher numbers yielding the better rate and loan terms. Although just three digits, these numbers can set you on top of the borrowing heap or take you lower than a whale's belly button. These numbers are taken from an average of what the rest of the borrowing world has done when paying back their obligations, and more importantly, what you have done with your current obligations.

I have heard some investors voice concerns that too many inquiries on their credit report can lower their score. I understand their concerns, but do not let this issue stop you from shopping around for the best loan, as your score is only minimally affected through inquiries that occur around the same time. Lenders will understand that you are shopping for the best rates. Lenders use the scores to do the same thing you have to do when dealing with investments—that is, to mitigate risks. Lower scores generally come with some type of risk premium, which can mean you have to pay more.

Your score is not your score for life—the numbers fluctuate. However, you want your scores to always be above the 700 mark because a number at least that high will yield you great lending options. If you do not know your score, you can go online to Equifax, Experian, or Trans Union to see how they rank you. These companies are also available by phone. Their contact information is listed here:

Credit Service	Web site	Phone Number
Equifax	www.equifax.com	1-800-685-1111
Experian	www.experian.com	1-888 397 3742
Trans Union	www.transunion.com	1-877-322-8228

I would also recommend that you have a look online at some of loan calculators. There are many good Web sites out there, but using the sites listed above should prove to be more than sufficient. There are calculators for loans of many types including mortgages, cars, retirement, and personal loans. These sites have questionnaires set up to give you a guide on where you might stand when trying to borrow money from banks and other lending institutions.

Banks are not in the business of buying and selling real estate. They are in the business of lending money at a profit. They understand the time value of money and how to use leverage to get more out of what they have. The time value of money basically means that a dollar today is worth more than a dollar tomorrow. Fifty dollars in 1950 went a lot further than fifty dollars today because inflation eats away at its value.

You may want to think of it in terms of your retirement plan. Traditional 401(k)s and IRAs are funded today for a future value many years from now. When you make contributions, the money grows due to compound interest or interest paid on the principal and the interest. When banks lend you money for mortgages, the same compound interest is at work. The issue is, in this situation you are on the opposite side of the equation. When you contribute to your retirement plan, compound interest works for you, but when you take out loans, it works against you. So once the banks have lent the money to you, they can make loans to others because the money that you are paying back to them primarily goes to the interest first. By the time you really begin making a dent in the principal, the bank has already received quite a bit of money from you in the form of interest. Therefore, they have leveraged your money to make even more.

Finding the right mortgage can be as important as investing in the right property. In some cases, the mortgage can be more important than the property. If you do not find the right mortgage, you may end up paying way more in interest than you had to, which means that you significantly delay your opportunity to gain valuable equity in the property. You have to read the fine print: if you have a mortgage that you do not understand and a change in payment hits you unexpectedly, you can find yourself in hot water in a hurry.

There are more types of mortgages than I care to talk about, and I am not a mortgage loan officer, but many people commonly think of thirty-year fixed mortgages when buying homes. It is one of the safest loans you can have. However, as an investor, a thirty-year fixed mortgage may not be the one you are most interested in. You are probably not looking to keep a property for thirty years, and while it is not unheard of for people to pay off investment properties, you do not want to be the person to do it.

Instead, your renter's timely payments and your good investment strategy should pay off the mortgage if you want it paid off. If you find yourself with a property that you decide to keep for thirty years, it is probably in a very good location, and more than likely, it is generating good revenue. Personally, I do not have a property that I would want to keep for thirty years, and I do not have any investor friends who do. In all, I think it is better to pick a mortgage that is more in line with your investment goals than a thirty-year fixed mortgage.

For example, if your plan is to hold on to the mortgage for just a few years and then sell the property, an interest-only loan may be more appropriate. With this loan, your principal balance—the amount that you initially borrowed—will stay the same provided you don't make any additional payments, but you can keep your payments low for the first few years. If your property is generating positive cash flow after you have paid all the monthly obligations, more money can go into your pocket. When you sell the property in a few years, while your balance may be the same, the benefit is that your monthly expenses were lower. The idea is to allow the property to increase in value over the years and profit off the sale with the least expense possible.

Let's look at the following example. Listed below are two $100,000 loan scenarios for the same property. These payments do not account for taxes, as tax rates will vary across the country. One is a 7 percent, thirty-year fixed and the other is a ten-year interest-only loan. On the thirty-year fixed loan the payment is $665.30 a month. Although it is a higher payment, the overall balance is steadily decreasing. At the end of ten years, the balance on the thirty-year fixed payment is $85,812, which is a difference of just under $15,000.

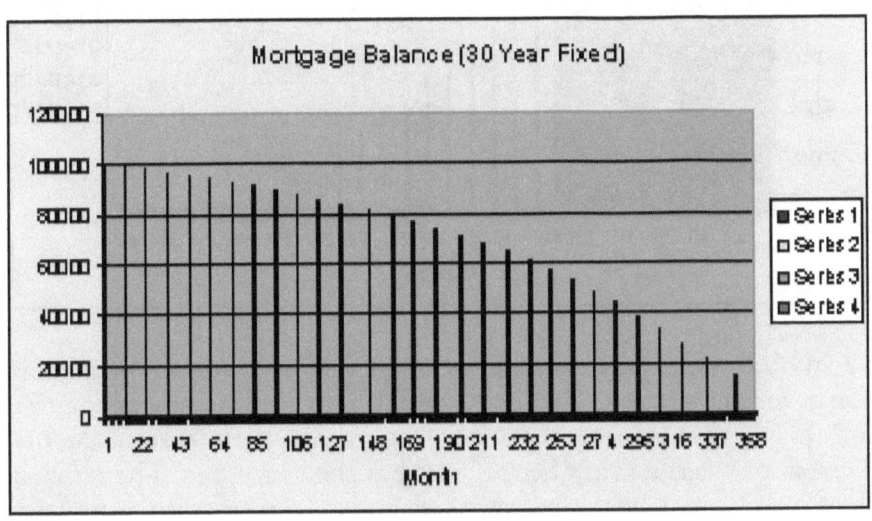

On the ten-year interest-only loan, the payment based on a 7 percent loan is $583.33 a month. Over the first ten years, the balance remains the same. In the meantime, you are pocketing an additional $82 a month—or just under $1,000 a year—that can be invested elsewhere. If you invested that $1,000 a year in the stock market with a 12 percent return (average is 12–14 percent which is commonly known and accepted in the world of stocks and mutual funds), the value of that savings would be $19,655. In this scenario, not only have you lowered the monthly payment but you will have been able to accumulate nearly $5,000 more just for picking a better loan option. The $15,000 above is the amount that you paid down the principal on the thirty-year loan over the ten-year period. But, the $1,000 a year saved on payments by using the ten-year interest-only loan, plus the 12 percent investment rate, totals it to a savings of about $19,655. You save about $10,000 by using the ten-year interest-only loan, plus gain $9,655 by investing that $10,000 in the meantime. To see more on monthly mortgage payments you can go to any number of financial websites and access their online calculators. I have chosen bankrate. com for this exercise.

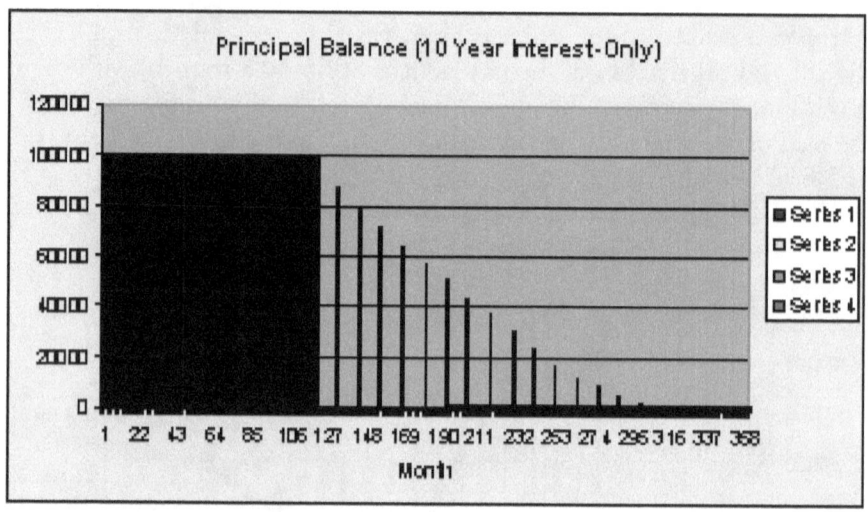

With interest-only loans, as with many other nontraditional loans, you have to be concerned with rate or payment adjustments. In interest-only loans there are several choices. You may have an interest rate that is fixed for a certain number of years but then increases. The terms of the fixed rate may be three, five, or as many as ten years. In some cases, the loan can adjust sharply, leaving the loan holder to make a much higher loan payment.

** Something to think about

I purchased my first home in July of 1998 for $108,000. I knew little to nothing about the mortgage or real estate industry. When I arrived at the closing table, I was expecting to sign documents that showed the $108,000 price tag, but instead the documents showed $296,000. My eyes must have about popped right out of my head. I gasped and said, "Hey, what is this? My house only cost $108,000!" The closing agent looked at me and said, "I know that." "I replied, "Well then why does the document state $296,000?". Grinning and acknowledging my youth she said, "Oh, that's how much you will pay us over the next thirty years with interest". I said, "But the interest is double the price of the house". Still smiling she said, "Yeah, I know." Compound interest can be a beautiful thing but it all depends on if you are on the receiving end or the paying end.

The best advice I can give is to find a lender you can trust that is willing to sit down with you and discuss the full life cycle of the loan. Only then will you truly understand what you are getting. Work with a reputable bank. There are many banks that can be found on the Internet, and some investors feel that they should not be as concerned with the bank itself as they are with what the payment on their loan will be. This is a bad mindset to have. Regardless of what you are doing, you get what you pay for.

If you find that local banks are not willing to approve you for a loan you desire, then they may be doing you a favor. Some Internet banks are out to cook their books to make you look desirable to an underwriter. They charge expensive hidden fees, and as long as you have no customer service questions or concerns before the loan is sold to investors, you may get away unscathed. However, when you find that you need questions answered and your loan officer is two thousand miles away with no local branch in sight, getting the proper attention can become very difficult.

More often than not, your loan will be sold to another lender. Lenders sell mortgages to other lenders for many business reasons. For one, it can free up their debt so they can make more loans. As we discussed with the time value of money, lenders can hold the loan and collect the series of interest payments over the term of the loan, or they can sell it today for a profit and find other uses for the money.

A lot of these decisions will depend on the state of the mortgage industry. We have to also keep in mind the value of Wall Street in the mortgage market. The Unites States economy is heavily affected by the mortgage market, as we are seeing in recent years. Lenders have thousands and even millions of dollars in interest payments that they receive every month. That type of money catches the eye of large investment banks. They know they can make substantial profits from month to month with those payments, so lenders are willing to sell the loans to investors. Mortgages can be sold in bundles to large investors who will then resell those mortgages as securities, hence the name "mortgage-backed securities." Those securities are backed by your mortgages and can be sold to the same mutual funds that hold your 401(k)s.

So as you can see, the payment of your mortgage not only provides a roof over your head but can also provide a nest egg for your retirement. This is why I recommend real estate investors to not turn a blind eye to Wall Street. After all, your retirement plan is not stuffed with property addresses, but with stocks and bonds instead. For much more on the subject of selling mortgages, I highly recommend the book *Mortgage Confidential* by David Reed.

As an investor, the last thing you want is to find yourself in a position where you cannot get good information from the people you owe money to. Remember that real estate is usually a local business, so it is probably better to work with a local bank. I find that they are aware of local conditions and can be very insightful about your investment goals.

From beginner investors to seasoned billionaires, I have heard all kinds of people talk about the benefit of working with local lenders when times get difficult. Their reasoning for this is that if you have a good track record of doing business with a local bank and you find yourself in a difficult time, your bankers are often willing to renegotiate terms to help you out. They want to help you succeed, as lenders are not in the business of selling property. If they can find a way to help you keep the property, they would prefer that over foreclosure. It is much easier for them. More important, it is much more lucrative for them to help you work through your payment troubles than to have you default on your mortgage. Chances are your problem is temporary, even if it seems like it takes you a long time to recover. The lender would not have given you the loan if they thought you could not repay them. They understand that bad things happen to good people.

Who should hold the mortgage?

I had to take a class on taxes at Georgetown University before I could finally get a good answer to the above question, from an instructor. Thank goodness for me he was a qualified tax attorney. I'm sure your situation will vary, but according to his experience, you *do not* want properties in your name. If that's the case, some of you may now be wondering, whose name should be put on the loan application?

You can put your name on the application and even put the property in your name. However, I would recommend you switch your name out soon after by titling the property under an LLC. LLC stands for "limited liability company," which is a common designation for small businesses. An LLC does just as the name implies, which is to limit your liability.

As much as I love America, one thing I have found is we may be the land of the free, but we're also the home of the lawsuit. If a man can take a local dry cleaner to court for hundreds of thousands of dollars over a pair of pants (true story), then someone can certainly take you to court for a slip and fall on an unsecured stone on your property.

When you have investment property, you have to be aware that renters may look at you as rich or wealthy, and some can be devious. You have to look out for number one—yourself. You protect yourself and by having your property placed under an LLC. An attorney can set this up for you. This is why I recommend you have an attorney as a part of your real estate investment team.

In the unlikely event some bloodthirsty tenant decides to take you to court for something trivial, their lawyers will want to know if the case is worth their time. If you have no assets, they will probably deem the case a waste of their time, as there is nothing to gain. However, if they run a simple search and realize that you have one, two, or maybe even three investment properties, they are much more likely to take on the case. There may be hundreds of thousands of dollars in equity just waiting to be won. But if you have the properties under an LLC, they will not show up under your name.

By far the best introduction to this topic I have seen that highlights asset protection comes once again from the king of the real estate game, Mr. Donald Trump. Trump has written the foreword for a book that I highly encourage you to read. The book is called *Asset Protection 101* and was written by J. J. Childers. Childers covers things such as whether your primary residence should be placed in a business's name, which he emphatically answers no. For starters, you would lose the mortgage interest that helps you heavily at tax time. Instead, he recommends your home be placed in a revocable living trust to avoid probate. If this is your first time hearing those words, probate is legal speak that means if you die without a will, the courts will decide what to do with your assets—and I assure you that they are the last people you want dividing up your things. The trust allows you to pass the assets on to your heirs without the courts intervening. You will also gain substantial tax advantages by doing this.

Childers's book also covers why you should set up holding companies as additional layers of protection to keep dishonest lawyers away from your hard-earned investments. I will admit that many of these strategies are for people who have income-producing properties or properties that have significant amounts of equity in them. What's a significant amount? That's up to you. If the amount that you have is significant enough for you to be concerned should you lose it, then you want to protect it. Childers believes in the school of John D. Rockefeller, who would be the richest man in the world if he was alive today. Rockefeller believed one should "own nothing but control everything." Here here!

Purchasing real estate and watching your assets grow is extremely exciting. Your assets can grow to seven figures faster than you ever thought possible, and placing the word "millionaire" after your name happens faster than you may think. You should work doubly hard to ensure that you learn about asset protection, estate planning, and other legal matters to keep your properties legally protected. You will be much wiser to learn these things now, before you encounter any problems. Cover your *A$$ets*!

The Power of Home Equity

LEVERAGE—The use of various financial instruments or borrowed capital,
such as margin, to increase the potential return of an investment.
—http://www.investopedia.com/terms/l/leverage.asp

Having equity in a home simply means that your house is worth more than you owe on it. If you have a home that is worth $75,000 but you owe $50,000, you have $25,000 in equity. Many American families have substantial wealth tied up in their homes. Some homes that have been paid off for years are worth hundreds of thousands of dollars, which puts such families in very strong financial positions. Equity in homes can be borrowed, and in many cases the proceeds can be tax free and the interest can be tax deductible. Please consult a tax advisor for more information on this topic, because individual results may vary.

Homeowners can build substantial wealth if they can wisely take advantage of the equity in their homes. On the same note, equity used carelessly or without a proper understanding can spell disaster. The reason is that lenders are willing to allow homeowners to borrow tens and hundreds of thousands of dollars at once. Many people are not accustomed to receiving that much money at one time. Some people act as if they have just won the lottery and their obligation to pay the money back is distant from their minds. Keep in mind that when you use your home equity, you do have to pay it back.

Home equity can give a person a feeling of being rich even when the money is still borrowed. Some take the OPM (other people's money) mentality that they have heard of and use it the wrong way. I have seen homeowners take out home equity loans for hundreds of thousands of dollars just to go Christmas shopping. My guess is that their families are very grateful for the generous gifts, but for many people, borrowing against their home equity for this purpose may be a bit excessive. I have seen others use home equity money to buy things they would not have normally bought.

If you do take out home equity, I would be very cautious of creating new bills. For example, if you take out $10,000 in home equity and make a purchase that creates an additional monthly obligation such as leasing a new car, you will now have two bills—the home equity loan and the new purchase. I cannot stress enough the importance of being responsible.

On the other hand, I have seen homeowners use home equity to make other investments that helped to start income-generating businesses. If you are looking to build wealth, you certainly want multiple sources of income, and using your equity wisely can get you there. For example, some analysts are in favor of using home equity to buy stocks and other analysts are not. As a financial advisor, I would recommend that before you use your equity for investments, it is very smart to talk to a financial advisor or financial planner so they can help you make good investment decisions while alerting you of any tax consequences. I have used equity to make both real estate and stock investments, but because this book highlights the real estate business, I will talk only about the real estate.

My first investment came by way of organic growth in 2002. I define "organic growth" as turning a property that you have lived in into an investment property. In this case, I used a townhouse as my primary residence for several years, and then I rented it out to a tenant. I did this at a time when the Washington DC region was experiencing record growth in real estate, so property values were rising very fast. Many Washingtonians were making tens and in some cases hundreds of thousands of dollars in their sleep. Because I had grown up in rural South Carolina, I was not used to living in townhouses and did not want to make one a primary residence for very long. I wanted a single-family house, meaning a house detached from other houses.

I had several options that assisted me in making that happen. I had tens of thousands of dollars in equity at the time, and the options I considered are listed here:

Home Purchase Price	Home Value	Year of value
$108,000	$108,000	1998
	$130,000	1999
	$145,000	2000
	$160,000	2001
	$180,000	2002

Options
1. Sell the townhouse
2. Rent out the townhouse
3. Rent out the townhouse plus cash-out refinance
4. Rent out the townhouse plus home equity loan or home equity line of credit (HELOC)
5. Take out a home equity loan or home equity line of credit (HELOC)

The home I was interested in buying required a down payment of $23,000. If I chose option 1, I could have sold the townhouse and walked away with just over $64,000, calculated as follows:

$180,000
- $105,000   loan balance
- $10,800   (6 percent commission on $180,000 sale)
$64,200

** Something to think about

Please note that just because you have equity in your house does not mean a bank will automatically give you a home equity loan or line of credit. You must still qualify for the loan based on income, credit score, and other factors. Having the additional equity does make lending to you more desirable for the bank, but if the other essentials are not met, your loan can be denied.

Option 1

I could have put some of the proceeds from the sale of the home toward the down payment on the new home that I desired, and that would have solved my down-payment issue. Although many would have taken this option, I did not find it the most appealing because property values were continuing to soar. Selling the property would have meant that I would lose out on future appreciation, or increase in value. Plus, there is an IRS code that basically states that I could exclude up to $250,000 from the sale of my property if I met a few rules. Because of the $250,000 exclusion, I would avoid having to pay taxes on the profit I earned from the home sale. Please see www.irs.gov and search for Publication 523 for more on this code.

Option 2

I could have rented the home out to a tenant. At the time, rental rates in my area were averaging roughly $1,200 per month. My mortgage payment costs were slightly above $900 per month, plus an additional fee of $130 per month for homeowners' association (HOA) fees. I would have been able to rent the home and still have positive cash flow of $170 per month. That would have proposed a decent solution; however, I would still have to find a way to come up with the $23,000 required to write the contract on the new home I desired.

Option 3 and Option 4 (Combined)

I wanted an opportunity to keep the townhouse, which was continuing to appreciate, while also gaining money for the down payment on the new home I desired and having money left over to pay off some debt that I had previously acquired. Choosing option 3 along with option 4 was one option that would make this happen. Because I had quite a bit of money in equity, I could go back to the bank and ask them to refinance my home at a price of $135,000 which was the minimum amount I needed. This would pay off the loan balance of $105,000 and would give me a tax-free check of $30,000. I would now have the funds required for the down payment, with money left over. Refinancing would create a new payment that was about the same as my then-current payment. I was able to obtain the same payment because interest rates had decreased since I bought my townhouse, and I was able to take advantage of more money for less cost. I would still be able to take advantage of renting the home out and having a positive cash flow from the renter.

Option 3 and Option 5 (Combined)

This option would have achieved the same results as the previous option, but it would have created two payments. The first one would be my original mortgage payment. I would have then had a second loan, a home equity loan or HELOC, in the amount of $30,000. This option would yield the same results as the previous option except instead of having one payment this option would create two payments because I would now have two loans.

I eventually chose options 3 and 5 combined. That option gave me the power to have two properties that were increasing in value simultaneously. Option 4 could have achieved very similar results, the difference being I would have had a bigger loan. I was able to take advantage of the second home, which became my primary residence. It was appreciating at an even greater rate than my first townhouse because it was larger. That allowed me the opportunity to purchase several other homes and create several other streams of income by renting out these properties monthly and making a profit from each of them. One way to build wealth is to have multiple sources of income that eventually pay for your debts outside of your nine-to-five job.

As you can see, when used the right way, home equity can be a powerful tool. But to those who do not use it wisely, it can spell disaster by creating a lot more debt than you originally had.

A Trip to the County

Members of The Investment Forum's Venture Capital Group with David Byrd (center), deputy chief administrative officer for government operations/ environmental services, Prince George's County, Maryland.
Left to Right: Reggie Eleazor; Lori Bell; Robert McCauley; Von Mickle, president of The Investment Forum; David Byrd; LeVon Parrish; Paul Robinson; Lamar Brown; Carl Coppage; Sonya Coppage; and Bryan Royal

During the planning stages of a recent group investment for the National Harbor project located in Oxon Hill, Maryland, I decided to call Prince George's County executive Jack Johnson's office. I targeted the National Harbor because of its monumental impact on the Washington DC metropolitan area. This project had the makings of something that only comes to an area once or twice in a lifetime. The harbor is a multibillion-dollar initiative slotted to open in the spring of 2008. It will be the fifth most visited tourist destination on the east coast. It will contain five hotels boasting some two thousand hotel rooms. It will be the tenth largest hotel development in the world. The construction site has more cranes running than any place in the world outside of Dubai, United Arab Emirates, according to the Prince George's County Economic Development Corporation as of June 2007. With statistics like those, I knew it had the makings of a real estate deal that I wanted to be a part of. I didn't know all the details of what this project would offer, but I was willing to give any way I could get my team involved in the project a try.

I met Mr. Johnson in July of 2006 at a fundraiser for Kweisi Mfume in Potomac, Maryland, and through a detailed discussion, I was hoping to gain some insight into the National Harbor venture. To kick off this project, his staff agreed to meet with me and a representative number of The Investment Forum's members. It wasn't long into the meeting that I discovered this was definitely the right move.

The staff not only alerted us of the details of the National Harbor project, but they also told us about twelve other billion-dollar projects that would soon be coming to Prince George's County that we might have wanted to get involved with. In addition, they agreed to give us personal tours of the National Harbor project and one other project of our choosing. The meeting was granted by David Byrd, deputy chief administrative officer for government operations/environmental services and co-chaired by Kwasi Holman, president and CEO of the Prince George's County Economic Development Corporation. Patricia Thornton, director of marketing, was also in attendance to discuss new initiatives in the international trade zone.

These two fine men and this woman gave us a wealth of information about the county, not only from an economic development standpoint, but also about many other topics. We never would have gained this detailed insight without their help. Several other members of the executive staff were also on hand to provide us with insight into a multitude of things. From an investment standpoint, I can assure you that starting here was certainly the right place.

Mr. Holman and Mr. Byrd also told us about an organization that we absolutely had to be a part of called the International Council of Shopping Centers (ICSC). This organization holds a mega event each year in Las Vegas to discuss what new developments will be coming to every major city in the world. It is an overwhelming event that contains details of new shopping malls as well as the stores that will be in and around them. You can visit ICSC online at www.icsc.org.

After the meeting, The Investment Forum began talking about several franchise opportunities that we thought would make viable investments in this gala new National Harbor project. I immediately began to entertain the idea of an ice cream franchise. I made a few calls and within a few weeks, I had an appointment with Cold Stone Creamery. When they asked about a desired location, I mentioned the National Harbor. They quickly explained to me that while my idea was good, my timing was late by three years.

I wondered how I could be three years too late. If this new development didn't have one complete building yet, I thought, surely I must be one of the first people to introduce the idea of building there to investors. In fact, many of the people I polled about National Harbor had not even heard about it. Regardless of what I thought, I had terribly underestimated commercial investors. The most intelligent and informed investors had visited the county office years ago and become acutely aware of investment opportunities that were not yet in sight.

As an investor in residential real estate, not only do you want to be acutely aware of what is around you, but you should also know what is coming. One of the few ways you are going to have the insight into what is coming is by visiting the county executive's office to get economic development information. Even if you find that the area in which you are looking to make your acquisition is already fully developed and has no superficial site for new development, you should visit anyway. New roads can eventually make their way through older neighborhoods as developers look to build new homes near existing communities. You will be much wiser to market your property for rent when you know what is coming than someone who doesn't have a clue.

You may gain key contacts from the economic development office or the county's government center. If anyone tells you about a project and the county executive's office does not know about it, then that is probably a bad sign. That new development could be in violation of a code or standard. When the county finds out about it, they may order the project to be stopped immediately. Although I have not had this happen to me, Mr. Byrd did mention several incidences of this sort of thing within Prince George's County.

If you purchase a property near a site that has not been cleared for development and the tenants sign a lease because they have heard about that development, you may be in for an uphill battle. If the county closes the site and tenants decide that this site was the only reason they leased the nearby place from you, they may want out of their agreement. This will leave you holding the bag—not only do you have a broken lease that you were hoping to receive revenues on, but prospective tenants may not want to take ownership near a project that has been condemned. One bad report could make it to all the local papers and television stations. With this type of image, you may now have substantial difficulty renting out the property, or even selling it.

You will find that some renters have lived in a particular area for years and are acutely aware of where they should not rent. Without an accurate assessment of the area you are seeking to invest in, you could find yourself with property that no one but you is interested in. This is where the importance of dealing with property management companies comes in, a topic that we will discuss more in a later chapter.

Stopping by the county's government offices to obtain planning and zoning information can be one of the most beneficial uses of your time before you spend any money. They can provide you excellent resources on other businesses in a certain area that may make your property more marketable. They are there to help make the county—and your business—a success.

Tax Assessments

Two things in life are certain, death and taxes.
—Benjamin Franklin

When you purchase property, you have to pay tax on the purchase price as well as property taxes every year that are levied by the county. In my tenure with investments, I have only seen taxes go up, despite what any politician has said about his plans if elected to office. You should know as much as you can about what taxes you will be responsible for. It is not enough to simply know what your mortgage payment will be and how much you should be able to rent your property for. In addition, try to find out how the tax rates have adjusted from year to year. You can get this information from the county government's office by asking about tax assessments.

**Something to Think About

I have heard many people assume that they can buy foreclosed properties for the taxes owed. While it is possible to buy a foreclosed property because someone didn't pay their taxes, the property won't appear on the foreclosure market overnight. Just as banks are not in the business of owning properties, neither is the county government, which collects real estate taxes. They would much rather work out a payment plan than foreclose on a property. When the county government forecloses, it is generally because the property owner simply gave up and refused all communication over an extended period of time. So while foreclosure can happen due to nonpayment of taxes, the mortgage company will probably foreclose before the county does.

When I purchased my first home, which was my only residence at the time, I felt good believing that my mortgage payment would never change—or so I thought. I had no idea that even though your mortgage may have a fixed rate, your payment can and probably will go up at some point. The reason for this is taxes. The money you owe on your mortgage consists of the amount that you have borrowed from your lender plus a risk premium (interest rate) and taxes. The mortgage company could be in your town or on the other side of the country. Either way, it does not control the taxes for your county.

Property taxes are controlled by the local government. You should pay close attention to your tax assessments each year, as these assessments will list what the county thinks your property is worth based on the last six months of home sales. If the average sales price has increased, so will your taxes. In markets where real estate suddenly appreciates more rapidly than expected and sellers make handsome profits, keep in mind that locals will receive much higher tax assessments because of the new sales prices. That means higher taxes for you.

Taxes are paid through escrow accounts managed by a third party and are generally levied semiannually. The bulk of your monthly mortgage payment generally pays off interest (based on the average thirty-year fixed loan) while the remainder pays off the principal and taxes. If the taxes owed increase—and they probably will—then you may have a shortage in your escrow account as the account had enough money to pay taxes at the lower rate, but not enough money to pay taxes at the higher rate. Mortgage companies can pay the extra money due, but you will be billed for the amount. The mortgage company will either ask for the entire shortage amount up front, or they can divide it into twelve payments, which are added to your monthly mortgage payment.

Here is an example of a tax scenario on a $100,000 mortgage. This is used for illustration purposes only—your situation may vary.

January 1, 2007
Property value—$100,000
Monthly payment—$845
     $665 goes to interest, $100 goes to taxes, and $80 goes to principal.
Semiannual taxes—$600
Mortgage—30-year fixed, 7 percent interest

For the second half of the year, your taxes go up due to increasing property values.

July1, 2007—Higher tax assessment due to increasing property value
Property value—$100,000+
Monthly payment—$895
     $665 goes to interest, $150 to taxes, and $80 to principal.
Semiannual taxes—$900
Mortgage—30-year fixed, 7 percent interest

In this example, the taxes for the year *would have been* $1200 ($100 a month × 12 months). Since the taxes went up halfway through the year due to higher property values in the neighborhood, the semiannual taxes went to $900. Based on the current mortgage payment, you will be short by $150 for half the year and $300 for the entire year. The mortgage company will either ask you for the difference up front or divide it into twelve equal payments and tack that onto your mortgage. In this example, that is an additional $50 per month. Your new mortgage payment will be $895 instead of $845. So as you can see, even though your interest rate stayed the same, your mortgage payment increased.

Once I was given a tax surprise on three investment properties at the same time through a sales agent's miscalculations and my lack of follow-up with the county. Because of the agent's miscalculations, I had three escrow shortages and was sent three very large tax bills. I assure you that you don't want to be the unsuspecting receiver of multiple tax bills at the same time.

This is a mistake I should not have allowed to happen, as I had experienced this with my first property and should not have allowed it to happen a second time. No one warned me about tax increases when I purchased the property. Perhaps the people I trusted felt it wasn't their responsibility or thought I already knew. I assure you that unless you have a good team around you, there are a lot of surprises out there. When you ask people after the fact, they often give you that dumbfounded look that says, "I thought you knew."

**Something to think about

Escrow shortages can catch investors off guard and eat away at their profits. When you have long-term (for one year or more) rental agreements that have a stated amount, you want to charge your tenants enough to cover an unexpected escrow shortage. If you cannot pay the escrow shortage amount, you will have a new, higher mortgage payment that you may not be able to cover strictly with the rent you receive. For this reason alone, do not be in a rush to acquire properties. Take your time and allow the business cycle to unveil itself.

Another surprise I discovered had less to do with taxes and more to do with the "eighth wonder of the world," as Albert Einstein purportedly called it, or compound interest, as it is more commonly known. To avoid making this into a complex mathematical discussion, I just want to mention that for the first several years of many mortgages, the vast majority of your money is paid to interest. You do not begin to noticeably knock down the principal for many years. Your loan is front-loaded with interest so the mortgage company can get their money back for providing you the loan. I was not aware of this until I sat down at the closing table to sign off on my first home.

The sales price of that home was $98,000. I added $10,000 in options, making the total price of the home $108,000. When I began to sign the documents, I noticed a much different number. The figure was nearly $300,000. I told the closing agent to stop. When she asked what was wrong, I told her I thought she had the wrong house. She then explained to me that the numbers were correct and that after thirty years, $300,000 was how much I would have paid, with interest. It was a very shocking lesson to learn that I should have known about long before sitting down at the closing table.

Months later when I began studying 401(k)s and how money grows to substantial amounts over time, I wondered again how such a small amount would become such a large amount. The answer was, once again, compound interest.

Assembling a Team

"Foundation of Excellence"

Tentative efforts lead to tentative outcomes. Therefore give yourself
fully to your endeavors. Decide to pay the price of a worthy goal. The
trials you encounter will introduce you to your strengths. Remain
steadfast ... and one day you will build something that endures;
something worthy of your potential.
—Epictetus, Roman teacher and philosopher, AD 55–135

When you decide to take on a new venture and you are
determined to be successful, be prepared to get knocked
down multiple times—sometimes hard—even when you
think you are up and running. When you are looking for ultimate
success, you set out on a path of great resistance. You have to leave your
comfort zone, and your brain has to learn to do new things and think
about things you have never faced before. It can be very frustrating,
but you can't quit. There are many times in life when you will find it
best to go it alone. Real estate investing is not one of them. Not only is
it not a good idea to work without a team, you simply cannot do it.

From lenders to closers or inspectors to maintenance guys, you
will need the help of a competent team. This should be a team that
knows you and what your goals are. It is okay to not have this team

completely assembled at first, as you probably will not know enough people. But as your portfolio grows, it is a lot easier to have a team that you can call when you encounter a potential investment than it is to have to handle everything yourself.

The most important member of your team should be your mentor. Hopefully this is someone who has experienced both success and failure. Knowing how to effectively deal with things that don't go how you planned is critical because you are sure to find yourself in such situations at some point along the way.

This is where I am critical of many of the best-selling books on real estate I have come across. Many of these books only highlight the good times. That is super for book sales and motivation, but it is hardly the whole picture. When you encounter a problem as a result of something you read in one of these books, you will quickly see why it is important to have someone that you can reach out to for help. Calling Donald Trump for further understanding of something you read in his book is nearly out of the question, although well worth a try. You never know.

Trump lives a life that many of us dream of. As a kid, I knew he was rich and a big businessman, but I didn't even know he was a real estate tycoon. All I saw was his larger-than-life lifestyle. I have read that he had four hundred million dollars the day he was born thanks to a very hard-working father. I have also read that he received one-hundred-million-dollar loans while he was in his twenties. If that's the case, then I'm happy for him. He was blessed to have such a great and well-off dad. But the rest of us simply are not that fortunate. Note that I do not say these things in a negative way, as I am a big fan of The Donald.

Even Trump realizes the importance of having a team. As much as he seems to love himself, I have yet to see him go it alone on any real estate venture. If he needs a team, then I assure you that you will need the same.

I have been extremely fortunate to find a mentor who has many more years of quality experience than I have. I have taken great refuge in a beautiful soul named Shirley Dominick. She has been instrumental not only in my real estate growth, but in the growth of many of my colleagues. I have been able to run many scenarios by her, and she is always willing to listen and provide insight. One of the things I appreciate most and that is very important for me is that she comes from humble beginnings and has soared to substantial heights. All the while, she has stayed very much grounded, and I never get the feeling

I am being talked down to. I only wish I had met her sooner in my ventures.

There are other Shirley Dominicks out there, but do not expect people to just come out and pour loads of knowledge into your head about the future. You will have to tell people what you are doing. As long as you speak with confidence and demonstrate that you are serious about your success, you will be surprised just how much people with experience are willing to help you. I would recommend this as a very good way to find a mentor of your own.

Ray Porter, a Citadel alumnus and colleague of mine in the technical arena, did very well investing in a number of properties in northern Virginia. He admitted to me that he owed his success primarily to a team he assembled consisting of a real estate agent, mortgage broker, insurance agent and attorney. He mentioned to me a deal that he was introduced to was closed on and sold at a profit within a matter of days. This gentleman profited tens of thousands of dollars from that sale. He had a team in place that understood his resources and his goals, and when presented with the opportunity, he was able to pounce on an opportunity at a moment's notice.

> ****Something to think about**
>
> Your team may include—but not be limited to: a real estate agent, an attorney, a CPA, a property management company (if necessary), an insurance agent, a banker, and a contractor. Your team can be your guide to future deals once they have an understanding of your resources and what your investment goals are.

The first two homes that I lived in were purchased new. I knew exactly where I wanted to live and knew the type of home I wanted. In both experiences, I had no knowledge that I would purchase a home on the day I did.

I have found that this phenomenon is not unusual, by the way. It is not unusual because some people like to visit new home communities simply as something to do. Many others visit new homes as a source of motivation, as they believe one day they will be in a position to obtain one of those homes for themselves.

If you ask the average person what their dream home looks like, they probably could not tell you. However, ask them to show you their favorite model, and they will take you straight to it. People's dreams require details that are often found in other people's creations, so visiting a model helps to add the details people couldn't figure out on their own. Do you know what your dream home looks like? Chances are you do not because you would never think to turn a junky old closet into a sauna or a garage into an upscale-looking apartment. However, once you see these types of details in a new home, you'll probably want it.

The "new house smell" doesn't hurt, by the way. When people who have no intentions whatsoever to purchase a home are able to see something tangible that they really like, they tend to ask themselves more action-oriented questions as opposed to making negative, passive statements. For example, instead of saying, "I can't afford it," which is very negative and passive, they will ask, "How can I afford it?" When the question is stated that way, people's minds begin to turn, and with a lot less effort than they realize, they obtain what they are looking for.

This process bodes well for new home sales and the real estate market in general. It keeps people involved in the real estate business, and as a real estate investor you want a market that is full of action, meaning both buying and selling.

At any rate, new homes have new-homes sales agents on hand, as you may recall from earlier chapters. To me, these agents served the same purpose as a real estate agent. As someone in the market for a personal residence, not having an agent for a new-home sale may not be a terrible thing. As an investor in unfamiliar territory, I would highly recommend having an experienced agent. In fact, it would serve you well to have an agent who is also an investor, as many of them are.

After I purchased my first few investment properties on my own, I decided to enlist the help of an agent named Jae Kim. This man was very sharp. He was technically savvy and had a team of people who supported him. He did more business in weeks than many agents did in years. This alone made him substantially more aware of the general geographical area than I ever could have been.

As I spoke to him more, I found out that I wasn't the only person going it alone. He told me about another gentleman who had purchased four homes over more than twenty years and how he overpaid for all of them. But with Kim's help as an agent, this man purchased more than twenty homes over the next four years, all with very good profit margins. Success in this business—or any business, for that matter—can rely on the realization that while you may be smart at a lot of things, you are not the smartest at everything. It just makes more sense sometimes to let the experts do their jobs.

You want to establish a good working relationship with a bank. There are a significant number of people in the real estate business, and although I do not recommend that you operate in a rushed manner, sometimes you will have to move confidently and swiftly. If you have an established relationship with a bank, you can simply call your banker and give him or her the address of each property you find. The banker can go to work by getting all the essential information he or she needs to get your loan started. If you don't have this type of relationship and you find a property of interest, you will have to start the loan process from scratch each time. With thousands of competitors out there, you have to have a process that works.

As mentioned in an earlier chapter, establishing a good relationship with your bank helps in troubled times. If you have a good relationship and have worked together on multiple deals, bankers can give you more favorable decisions when markets turn against you. I recently came across a gentleman who owned nine hotels. Needless to say, he had done very well for himself over the years. But following the trials of September 11, 2001, his success started a rapid decline. September 11 left many people scared to fly. When people don't fly, they don't need hotel rooms. The lack of demand put this gentleman in a less-than-desirable situation.

As time pressed on, this man was unable to maintain his hotels. One by one, he lost them. When he came down to the last hotel, the bank wasn't sure what to do with it. The market wasn't particularly strong, and the bank needed to get rid of it. The man decided to break the hotel into two separate businesses, with one half being a hotel and the other being an upscale condo building. He asked the bank if they would finance the building for him until he could get the project completed. They agreed, and eighteen months after the work was done, he sold the building for a multimillion dollar profit.

There are a couple of notes to be taken from this story. One is that this gentleman had an entrepreneurial, never-give-up spirit, which is essential if you are looking for great wealth and success. The other is that he understood the value of having a great relationship with his bank. I'm quite sure that he would never have gotten the bank to finance this deal had he not shown a good track record over the years or if he had not given the bank business on the other hotels. I'm glad to say that today this serial entrepreneur has made a full recovery and is back in business as the creator of a budding franchise.

I also recommend that you enlist the help of a CPA. You can use a CPA for a lot more than just filing your taxes. A qualified CPA who understands your goals for building wealth can point you to the right places to invest. No matter who you go to, good people know others who can help you.

Additionally, if you are having trouble finding other key members of your team such as bankers and agents, a good CPA can point you in the right direction. CPAs can point you to attorneys that specialize in working with investors on a number of different types of investments. They can also help you in setting up the right entities for the most efficient tax strategies. For example, a CPA may tell you to organize your business as an LLC (limited liability company) or as an S corporation. You don't ever want to avoid paying taxes, but you do want to pay only what you owe. A CPA working for you as a tax strategist can help you minimize taxes in places you probably never thought of.

CPAs know who has money and who doesn't. They can see exactly where successful people make their money and how much they make. You will find that successful people often run investment deals past their CPAs to gain insight on what the tax consequences of those deals may be. If a deal is too small for more advanced investors, the CPA can run it past you as a potential investment. They want you to be successful, and they know what works and what doesn't.

The Investment Forum contains many real estate investors, and we often talk about lenders. When I found that we all used different lenders, I decided that we could have much better rates if we all decided to work with one lender. I set out to find a lender that would work for everyone. It just so happens that a new bank was being started by one of the most successful entertainment entrepreneurs the United States—and certainly the African American community—has ever seen. He is billionaire Robert Johnson, founder of Black Entertainment Television (BET).

I caught up with Mr. Johnson in September of 2006 to discuss hedge funds and other Wall Street investments. Our conversation soon led me to the grand opening of his newly formed Urban Trust Bank. Today the forum has a working relationship with the bank, and the entities are attempting to form a union that allows them to take advantage of real estate investments and build wealth in the years to come.

**Something to think about

I have come up with a solution to help you along the way. It is called the High Impact Presentation Tool, or HIP for short. The HIP is a DVD that illustrates how to connect with highly successful people by creating highly effective presentations that request their time. It is a proven method that has worked for over twelve years to help get people in front of highly valued, highly respected, and high-net-worth people. It has opened the doors to powerful and successful people with millions and even billions of dollars.

One of the principles discussed on the DVD actually got me a response from the office of "The Donald" to give me the okay to print his name in my book. How's that for displaying that it really works? You can get your copy of the High Impact Presentation DVD for $24.99 online at http://www.vonzforum.com/HIP.html.

Finding the Right Community

Location, location, location ...

Locating the right community to invest in can largely depend on what your strategy is for making the investment. If you are seeking to "flip" the property, which this book is not geared toward, then your community may be different from the community where you are looking to buy and hold for over a year. When seeking the right community, there are a number of things to consider.

Proximity. Renters like to be close to life's amenities. I would not advise buying a five-acre ranch forty-five miles outside of town in hopes that you will find renters. A renter will use your property for an indefinite amount of time, and then they are off to some other location. If your property is not convenient, the odds of it staying rented are limited.

This is not to say that you have to buy a property right in the heart of town, either. While the occupancy rates for downtown living are higher than those of the suburbs, it is not always the best investment to buy downtown. The competition you face with other properties for rent is much greater, and you may have to compete with landlords who make major updates, such as replacing carpet or painting, more frequently than you can. There is nothing wrong with these updates, but they are much more noticeable in urban areas. Your tenants may begin to ask you to uphold similar standards.

HOAs. Homeowners' associations come in all shapes and sizes. An HOA can add much-needed amenities to an otherwise drab community. Also, it can add a level of protection by enforcing standards that will keep a community looking good for years to come, which can make it attractive to renters. Let's face it; although we want our neighbors to be as tidy as ourselves, some people are absolute slobs. So in helping us love our neighbors as ourselves, homeowners' associations can keep neighbors' properties intact without you having to knock on the door. Some communities are very strict and leave very little to chance in having residents disturb the developer's masterpiece.

Homeowners' associations can begin with the best of intentions, but not all of them enforce their rules to the fullest extent. My experience has been varied. I have had communities where they allowed satellite dishes but were very particular about where you were allowed to place them, which is very annoying. Other times I have had associations tell the residents they could not park junk cars around the property, which was good for property values. As an investor, the last thing you want to deal with when trying to rent or sell your home at maximum profit is having a potential buyer get turned away because your neighbor won't move his junk car. Associations that are strict will send nasty letters at a moment's notice to discourage this and similar acts.

While HOAs can be helpful in keeping a community looking good, their fees can also eat into your profits. I have experienced this several times. In a lot of properties it is difficult to stay out of the red during your first rental year. An HOA fee can be the expense that keeps you out of the black. Depending on the level of property you have—whether it is high-end, rapidly appreciating oceanfront or a normal townhouse rental—it can be a necessary expense. The HOA fee simply depends on what type of property you are trying to purchase and where you are making your purchase.

Investors welcomed? Regardless of profit, loss, or cash flow, some communities simply discourage investors and will not allow you to purchase. These are generally new-home communities that may be concerned about whether you are going to live there or not. Some communities will make mandatory standards that state the buyer has to live in the community for a certain amount of time before selling. Some will make regulations saying that no one can put for-sale signs in the front yard. The list goes on and on, and it depends on the real estate cycle and the area, because real estate is a local business.

Some established communities do not want their friends and neighbors disturbed. In these cases, if they find that you are looking to add tenants to your newly acquired property, the community will discourage you or, in some cases, not even sell the place to you. Buying a property may be a business transaction to you, but that property could mean significantly more, such as the place where someone's family was raised, to those who are not investors. A non-investor might not want the idea that the property stands for jeopardized with your desire to make a profit. Keep this in mind when you are looking to buy properties.

The Joneses. Pay attention to the communities when you enter them. Does everyone have freshly manicured lawns? If so, you should be prepared to keep up the appearance of your property's lawn. Do not expect the renters to care if the grass is cut or the flowers watered. You must realize that this is *your* property, whether you live in it or not. If the property has a lawn, you may even consider providing a lawn mower.

Some neighbors are very good at playing follow the leader. If one neighbor does something, the rest of the community will mimic him or her. Will it matter to you if your property is the black sheep of the community? Whether it matters to you or not, it will probably matter to the members of the community.

Finding the Right Property

Nothing takes the place of due diligence, as an ounce of advice is
worth a pound of experience.
—Annie R. Mickle, U.S. Army, retired

When seeking a good investment property, I would recommend beginning with the end in mind. If you are following the buy-and-hold, long-term approach, your goal is to rent the property out for a profit in the short term while seeking capital appreciation and tax benefits in the long term. Again, you want to ensure that you have a team in place to help you do this. The order of operations for this process is not intuitive, and I had to learn it the hard way.

Several years ago, I purchased an investment home because I thought it looked "rentable" and that the price was right for my budget. Excited about making the purchase, I did not implement the team approach or follow a process. Instead, I purchased the property out of emotion and excitement of making an investment. Wrong answer.

The house was built very well, but finding a renter was tough. I talked to two property management companies to find the type of renter I was looking for. After two months on the market without renters from the management companies, I eventually found a renter myself. This should not have taken so long, as the rental market at the time was strong.

There were a few problems that led to this situation. First, I picked a property management company that was not capable of finding who I was looking for. Second, I rented in an area that was less likely to attract a renter for the price I needed. Looking back I see exactly why I had a tough time filling the rental void. Today I use a much different approach.

Because I have several properties and keep many projects in the air, I have to rely on the services of property management companies. There is simply not enough time in the day for me to be consumed with the operational issues, so I have to start with the people who protect my bottom line—the property management company.

I recommend going to a property management company and asking what sections of the community are renting well and yielding the best returns on investment. The "best return" is not defined as how much money the house rents for. Just because one property rents for $1,600 a month and another only rents for $500 a month doesn't make the $1,600 property the better value. The more costly property may be located in a gated community with lots of upkeep costs and higher taxes, while the lower priced one may have a much higher profit margin.

You want a community where the renters have a high propensity to pay on time and keep your property in good shape. A good property management company knows the local area and has the experience and the statistics to know exactly what direction to point you in. I advise building a stronger relationship with the management company than perhaps with some of the other team members, as the company will have a continuing relationship with each particular property, whereas a real estate agent may only see you at the beginning of a deal.

Once the management company provides you with the areas you should focus on, I would then recommend utilizing the services of a good real estate agent to access some of the available properties in the community. The agent will be able to look up comparable properties and see what they have sold for at the past several closings. This is important so that you will be armed with good information when negotiating for a fair price.

In real estate, the value is set by the buyer. One week a property could be purchased for $80,000, and two months later it can be sold for $100,000 with no adjustments made to it and no obvious increase in real value. Someone who never saw the property marketed at $80,000 could be very willing to pay $100,000 any number of reasons. Perhaps a spouse or a child may *feel* like this is the one and encourage that it be purchased at whatever the asking price is. Multi-millionaire real estate investor Dr. Dolf de Roos said it best: "The deal of a lifetime comes along every week." In his book *Real Estate Riches*, he goes on to talk about a lot of simple and inexpensive things one can do to increase the value of a property.

You want your real estate agent to find a property that has already accrued equity instead of buying a property and hoping for it to gain equity over the years. The rental game can be tough if not played carefully because of a number of elements outside of your control. You want to ensure that you have room to refinance or sell any property should things go awry. We'll talk more about that during the chapter on exit strategies.

I recommend finding solid background information on at least five properties I believe having five or so properties that you perceive to be very solid investments will make you scrutinize which one is really the best deal. You may find more than one of them to be surefire successes. If that is the case, if it is available when you look to acquire another property, you will have already gotten a large part of your due diligence out of the way.

Please note, you may have to look at forty or fifty properties to get down to those five. At that point, you want to sit down and go back over all the pluses and minuses of each of the finalists. It is especially important that you shop around if you do not know the area or the market where you've been searching very well. Even seasoned investors shop around for the best deals, which is probably how they became seasoned in the first place.

When I make investments in mutual funds or individual stocks (which I don't recommend unless you truly understand how the company you're buying stock in makes its money and who their suppliers are, among other things), it amazes me whenever I listen to conversations from people who spend thousands of dollars on stock in companies they don't understand. The more mysterious the source of information about the stock, the more they buy. I'm almost willing to bet that if a blue leprechaun appeared in downtown Washington touting high returns on some high-tech stock, people would buy it in blocks.

That being said, I have seen real estate investors make purchases just as fast with just as little research. They buy because friends or relatives bought. I have heard stories of buyers making purchases because they heard some business that they think is good was supposed to be coming sometime in the future (could their information get any more vague?). The list goes on and on. The point is, you need to do some research before plunking down your hard-earned money. Do not buy the first thing you see. You have to be prepared to visit multiple communities and multiple properties.

Purchasing real estate is a business transaction. If you treat it as anything else, you may wind up in a lot of trouble. The house that you chose to live in may just "feel right," but I highly caution you to not take that approach to buying investment property. I have seen a lot of investors lose money because of emotion. Investing is a business in which you often have to leave your heart at home. Do not buy a property because it is pretty. At the same time, do not avoid a property because it is not pretty. You have to come prepared to make a business decision. If the property just happens to be pretty or whatever other adjective you'd like to use, then consider it a bonus. That suggests that this is not a decision you should rush into. If you ever feel pressure to buy, then you are probably doing business with the wrong people. Keep in mind that after you make the purchase, it is yours, and real estate is not a liquid asset. This means you can't sell it in a few days.

Although price alone may be tempting in some cases, I would never recommend that someone buy a property strictly based on price. Price alone does not tell the story of a property. Some things may be priced extremely high for what they are worth, while others could be priced extremely low. You may very well be able to get a good property for a song. However, you must still be aware that you get what you pay for, which goes back to the point that you shouldn't buy on price alone.

I knew someone who once bought an investment property because of its really low price. It wasn't long before he realized exactly why the price was so low. He didn't have a team to help him make informed decisions and as a result found himself in a property that he wished he could pay to get out of. Everything was wrong with it. The plumbing was horrible and required costly repairs. Structurally, the place was not built well. The foundation was weak.

In addition to the host of costly repairs required, it was in a crime-infested neighborhood. While he was trying to get the place ready for rental, local drug addicts kept breaking in to seek shelter for the night. This led to even more cost as he had to continuously repair doors and windows. Just the thought of all the trouble he had to go through regarding these repairs was worth him finding another place all together.

When making real estate investments, investors tend to buy because of the residual income made through appreciation and money earned in over and above the cost of the mortgage payment, such as through rent. Although some work is required, real estate is really a business where money is made while you spend your time elsewhere. If you have to spend ten or more hours per week checking the property for repairs, then you probably bought the wrong property. I made a $230,000 profit off one of my properties and I probably visited the place a total of five times over a three-year period for a maximum of two hours of my time, total.

Just as you are the buyer on a mission to buy, the seller is on a mission to sell. You have to remember what you are there for. Some sellers will understand the power of marketing and the little extra things to do to get you to make an offer. During my time at MHT, I witnessed a lot of builders' successes from the addition of an Otis Spunkmeyer oven to homes and a few dozen cookies. If you have never experienced an aroma that makes you hungry even after a full meal, you will experience that from the scent of these cookies. They are delicious and generally served hot. A seller can keep you viewing a property a lot longer than you think you had time for with the simple addition of a few warm cookies and a tasty beverage.

Should you buy properties new or used? Dr. Bob Pugh, my Keller Graduate School economics professor, says, "There is nothing better than a one-handed economist." That's because economists like to say things like, "On the one hand you've got A, B, and C. On the other hand you've got D, E, and F." The answer to the question above is, it depends. Remember, buying a property is a business decision. If the financials work out and you can make a profit with a newly built house, then by all means make the purchase. If the financials work with an older home already on the market, then buy that one. You are not looking to fall in love with the property; you won't be living in it, anyway.

I have purchased several newly built homes, and they all have their pluses and minuses. On the plus side, everything is not only new but is also under warranty. If anything breaks, usually within the first year, then you are covered. Simply place the 800 numbers in a cabinet in the kitchen, and the renters do not even need to get you involved. Another plus when buying a new home is that you have the opportunity to design it. You can spend extra money for things that you need, such as sturdy carpet, and downgrade what you do not, like having a gorgeous patio door. A basic patio door is as useful as a fancy one. However, buying cheap carpet and renting to people with small children will leave you with carpet that needs replacing sooner than you may like.

Buying a new house can often mean buying in a newly planned community. In a new community, there are a lot of people who have put in a lot more work than you have in making that community a success. You may have everything from convenience to a manicured entrance with lights and water displays. The lawns are fresh and the streets are new.

**Something to think about

If you buy new, do your homework on the builder. Just because your property is new doesn't mean it was built to last. Some builders build with what seem to be the cheapest materials they can find so they can maximize their profits. Some national builders have withstood the test of time and have repeat customers who stand behind the builders' products. Once I used a local builder, and while the property was very appealing to the eye, some of the craftsmanship was questionable.

I would also recommend that you check the builder's process and the customer service department. In fact, I'd recommend checking customer service before any major purchase. During the sale, the company can be very nice to you, but when it is time to file a complaint, a less-than-desirable builder may turn a deaf ear or blame anyone other than themselves. I have dealt with both local and national builders, and the bottom line is that you have to do your homework.

On the other hand (there's that economist again), buying new means any potential problems have yet to be discovered. You will not have any idea what the neighbors are like. Any problems with the home settling are as yet unknown. A nearby school's reputation may be one that tenants want or don't want.

By owning in an established community, many problems will have already been made known. You may not be burdened with all the things that come with a new home such as design, multiple walk-through inspections, and untested neighbors. Some investors only want to buy properties in seasoned communities, as they don't have time to wonder what will come out of a new development. Either way you decide to go, it is still a business decision.

You'd be surprised how much a digital camera or handheld camcorder can help when dealing with so many properties. Get organized, stay organized, and get to know your digital media. After you have gone through ten or fifteen houses, they can start to blend together. You may not know whether you liked the blue house with the white door and lightly colored kitchen or the green house with the dark door and dark-red kitchen. It can all blur in a hurry, so you will have to use technology that was designed to help you.

Technology, in this case, does not have to mean running out to your local retailer to get the latest and greatest gadgetry. To people who like to spend money, any excuse will do. Many people confuse technology with computing of some sort. While computers are definitely a part of technology, "technology" really means simply "a way of doing something better." Doing things better may not involve a computer at all. You would be surprised at the value a two-dollar writing tablet will add to your property search. A thorough analysis of handwritten notes can help you make a decision.

Another suggestion to help you find the right property is to take someone with you to see properties if at all possible. Two heads are better than one. A single guy may not know what it is like to live with a family, while a family guy may not know the desires of a renting bachelor. The more angles you have on potential renting arrangements, the better prepared you are to have success.

A word about inspection—your entire investment can be lost if you ignore this step. Investors who are just starting out generally have an untrained eye. Even investors who have been in the business for years can overlook details that can cause very expensive repairs. Do you know how much insulation is required in the attic per county code? Would you open bathroom cabinets and move items back under the sink to check for water leakage? Can you look at the roof and tell if it needs to be replaced soon? Chances are you do not have enough technical knowledge to inspect a property, and these are just a few items to think about.

The point is, when you are not fully aware of the things that are just below the surface, something as simple as an air freshener can pull blinders over your eyes. You should always enlist the services of an inspector, even if you are purchasing a new property. Many builders have inspectors who work for them and enforce tougher regulations than the local code, but you have to keep in mind that their inspectors are looking out for their partners' best interests. Who's looking out for you? It probably should be more than just you.

When making a purchase, negotiate. Negotiations take seconds. You can cut an asking price by thousands if you are willing and have the courage to put a number out there. Some sellers want to negotiate a price and have set an asking price with the thought that they will not get the full list price anyway. You don't have to take the price at face value in a normal market. If, however, the market has less supply than demand, you may not be able to negotiate.

Look to set an agreeable deal. Notice I never said to lowball a seller. While most investors intend to buy low and sell high to make a profit, you have to exercise caution. Buying low and selling high will occur naturally if you keep the property over time. If a person feels that you have gotten something from them for nothing, you can kiss your customer service or future business deals good-bye. Your business transaction can go sour very fast. If you are investing for the long term, be mindful of the reputation you build for yourself. You may get properties cheaply, but word-of-mouth goes farther and faster than any dollar.

Recommended essentials

Your team. I would highly recommend you bring as many members of your team as possible to see a property. As this can be a very drawn-out and time-consuming process, you don't have to bring them all at once. However, I would suggest you try to get them all involved at some point before the purchase.

Notebook. Not necessarily the computer, but the old-fashioned one with the lines on it in which you can actually write with a pen or pencil. If you do have a notebook computer, that is even better, and I highly recommend one for jotting down notes to refresh your memory.

Digital camera. I would suggest specifically a digital camera just in case your film prints do not come out right. With digital cameras, you get immediate feedback and can retake photos. You can also take multiple shots of the property from many angles without the thought of losing any film, because there is no film to lose. I would recommend creating a folder somewhere on your computer and naming it appropriately with the community that you are visiting.

If you do not own a digital camera, I would recommend visiting your local drugstore. They sell one-time-use digital cameras that take up to twenty-five pictures for less than twenty dollars. These cameras are very easy to use, and they even give you the nice digital display to instantly see what you have taken. The picture quality is extremely good for such a small investment.

Mobile phone. I would recommend bringing a cellular phone on any trip to a property you might buy. Usually there is some phone number attached to the property of interest, and if no one is immediately available to show it, giving a quick call may bring the magic key in moments. Even if the key holder cannot come for half an hour or more, he or she can call you when they are en route or you can call later if you are close by visiting another property. Using the address book feature is a definite plus. If you need the advice of someone on your team, having his or her number in the phone's memory will come in handy.

Clothing. Be sure to wear clothes that you do not mind getting a little dirty. Not all properties will be spick-and-span, so you probably won't want to wear your Sunday best. However, you do want to look professional since you are conducting business.

A list of comparable properties. Generally there is more than one property for sale in the neighborhood. You need to know how much comparable properties are selling for near the property you are looking to buy. Your real estate agent can look these up for you, or if you are searching alone, there are generally one-sheet advertisements of some form listed on the property.

Donahue Peebles has development assets worth billions of dollars. He hasn't worked for anyone in many years due to his successful real estate investing. His personal net worth is in excess of $500 million dollars. The Peebles Principles, he talks about the first property that he acquired, although, it was a large commercial office building, it provided him a yearly income of several hundred thousand dollars. At the time he wasn't even 25 years old. Later, Mr. Peebles developed Miami Beach's prestigious Bath Club which is his only residential project. Although most residential properties will not produce an income that strong, the value of his story is in the fact that he performed his due diligence and picked the right one the first time. Right at that moment, he was making the money he hoped he would one day make as a doctor.

The right property is your bottom line, and as you can see there is some work involved. Be sure to take your time and do most of your homework before venturing out. So many of the elements of finding the right property mentioned in this chapter can change fairly easily after the renting process has started, but your property remains stationary until you sell it. There is a chance you may have the property for five, ten, or twenty years, and while tenants will come and go, you want to ensure that your property stands the test of time. Selected properly, the right property can allow you to retire years in advance of when you'd ever dreamed due to great monetary appreciation and residual monthly income.

Nurturing the Landlord-Tenant Relationship

In God We Trust: All Others Pay Cash
—Title of a book by John Shepherd

I would certainly hope that you do your homework when selecting tenants. If you do, you can decrease the probability of problem tenants. But any tenant can become hard to deal with at times. The most important thing you should do is remain professional. Stay respectful when you are conversing, as you are not only talking to an adult, but also to a person who occupies a property that you own. The last thing you want to do is upset someone who has a key to your house!

**Something to think about
You will find that some renters want to use your property for six months, while others will want it for six years. There are some people out there who are lifetime renters and never want to own anything. It is important that you understand this concept when making an investment.

As an investor, you must remain aware that your mentality is probably different than that of a renter—and it should be. There is a strong possibility that if you own a rental home, you also have a primary residence. You are in the minority of homeowners because you have multiple residences. You think in terms of business, and you see things from a different perspective than other homeowners. You see property in terms of profit and not just a place for someone to lay their head. Since you excel in business, you are more apt to excel in other areas as well. Regardless of whether your tenants act ugly or not, you will always have to be businesslike and the bigger person.

When you have a tenant renting your property, you have established a relationship. These relationships can be good or bad, and that can largely be left up to you. As the landlord, you often set the tone of the relationship. Always be mindful that first impressions are lasting impressions. If you present yourself or your property to a tenant or potential tenant in a less-than-professional attitude, you are subject to get less respect, which could lead to less money. There are many horror stories about renters, but a strong relationship with a good tenant of a good property can be the cornerstone of a very prosperous relationship that will help ensure your wealth-building success.

Do not begin your relationship with your tenant by taking anybody's word for anything. If you have to agree to something, put it in writing. Before anything is committed to memory, it generally has to be said many, many times. If it bears repeating, then it should probably be written down. Be sure to keep good records of anything that has to do with your tenant or property.

Before you allow anyone to occupy your property, check their references. If possible, check three references from previous landlords. Eager to allow a new tenant to occupy a home I had purchased, I nearly overlooked the reference check due to several conversations and because the prospective tenant *seemed* nice and clean. Thankfully, before I signed any agreements, I did a reference check with his previous landlord. The landlord quickly told me what a mistake I'd be making if I allowed this individual to occupy my residence. He mentioned how the tenant had broken glass, trashed the yard, and left the home filthy.

Believe it or not, you *can* often judge a book by its cover. If you meet a potential tenant and he or she shows up not looking presentable, this person is showing you that what you see is what you get. Don't fool yourself into thinking that just because the tenant's car appears to not have been washed in two years, somehow he or she will keep the house clean and tidy. You can look at a person's front yard and tell exactly how they are living inside. If the yard is trashed, the inside of the house is probably a nightmare.

Checking a renter's credit can make the difference in you paying the mortgage for a tenant or them paying the mortgage for you. In some cases, bad things happen to good people. If someone has just gone though a divorce or unexpected serious medical condition, don't expect them to have a very good credit score. Conditions such as these tend to impair people's credit. You will have to make a judgment call. Look for signs of an extravagant lifestyle if a prospective tenant has a very poor credit rating. Have a conversation with them about their credit problems. If they can give you a legitimate reason why this problem is temporary and a solution to how it will be eliminated, be sure to take that into account.

**Something to think about

Don't underestimate the awareness of tenants. I have seen a lot of investors make the faulty assumption that renters rent because they cannot buy. I have even seen investors look at renters as second-class citizens, thinking that without the owner's property, a renter has no place to go. Let me assure you that you cannot make a more faulty assumption. The only thing you should assume about a renter is that they are looking to rent. Do not get involved in potential fallacies regarding social status or intelligence, as doing so will eventually lead you down a wrong and costly path. How renters or buyers view you could become very different. Once some people figure out that you are an investor with more than one property, they may immediately view you as affluent with no need for any further financial gain. Others may see you as just another investor looking to make a profit. Either way, you need to be knowledgeable about your area and the people you are dealing with.

However, just because a person with a less-than-great credit rating has some type of legitimate issue doesn't mean they should get a free ticket from you. Once credit has been tarnished, smart people realize that people with bad credit will have to pay more for the same goods and services if their credit is used. It is called risk premium. If your risk is low you pay less, and if your risk is high you pay more.

That said, you are not looking to charge one tenant $500 a month because they have good credit and another $600 a month because they have bad credit. You make up the difference in late charges. If a person has bad credit and you think they are worth the risk, give them an incentive to keep your mortgage payment a priority. In some cases, I have added late fees of up to 20 percent of the rental amount. A fee that heavy gets renters' attention, and if they are looking to rebuild their credit reputation, they will get their payments in on time. Of course, be sure to check your local laws regarding late fees, as some areas have a price cap.

When people have tarnished credit, they are often subject to not only higher interest rates and stiffer penalties, but also to sub-par service and respect. You don't want to take on a nasty reputation if you do business with someone who has a poor credit rating. Be disrespectful to them and they will oblige you by tarnishing your name. You can be firm without being rude. Just because someone has a less-than-stellar credit history does not mean that they deserve to be treated poorly.

Treat your tenant with the utmost respect and demonstrate that you respect your property in front of them. Seeing that you care about your things goes a long way to instilling respect for your things in the renter. It is wise to respect tenants, since they are occupying your residence, and you need them as much as they need you. They are your customers and you are in the customer service business. They are your fiduciary and stakeholder, so you want to treat them like it.

It is possible to have renters in a distant location, but you want to have a local support system to help you. I purchased several homes that were five hundred miles from where I live, but I was very fortunate to have Toni Boykin, a former middle school friend whom I came across again years later, to help me. Because this young lady was also involved in real estate, she was just as eager to assist me as I was eager for her help. She ran that entire multiunit operation. Fortunately for me, she and I worked well together, and I gave her full authority to act on my behalf.

Ms. Boykin became more familiar with the tenants than I did and always kept me informed of what was going on. Because we had a strong working relationship, the tenants began to trust her just as much as they did me. She lived only minutes away from the properties and was able to take an occasional look at how things were being maintained. That was a very rare experience for me, a young investor at the time.

If you do not have someone you know personally who can perform these tasks at a distant property, it is best to hire a property management company. They will be your eyes and ears while you are away. Be sure to interview several companies before you select one because they will represent you. To ensure a healthy relationship with your tenant, you need to know that you can count on the property manager you select to act in your best interest. If your tenants feel that they cannot trust or communicate effectively with your property management company, they may stop communicating, and that is something you surely do not want.

Always stay in touch with your renters. Some of my renters are on autopilot. They pay every month when required and never give me any trouble. They are clean and comfortable and are not looking to leave any time soon. That is a landlord's dream, and I can consider myself very fortunate to have them as tenants.

As much as that can be appreciated, you want to periodically check on your property. Always keep in mind that life has seasons and business has cycles. Even if nothing that requires your attention is happening now, you still want to keep a line of communication open. It is just good business for you and for your tenant. I do not recommend overdoing it, however, and I certainly would not mix business with pleasure. There is a line to walk when establishing a good tenant-landlord relationship.

When Problems Arise

I've had a lot of problems in my life, most of which never happened.
—Mark Twain

When investing in residential real estate, just like many other business ventures, you will encounter problems. Problems can stem from every angle that you thought possible, from every business group you have dealt with, at any time during your investment experience. As a business owner, you have to be prepared for problems, even at 3:00 AM. Show your tenants that you are not prepared to fix a leaky roof in the middle of the night, and they could show you how they are not prepared to give you your rent check at the end of the month. It is possible to put deductibles into the contract, which require tenants to pay for a portion of the cost of the repair.

Maintenance. Whenever you acquire a property, you should look as diligently for a maintenance person as you looked for the property. You should have someone who can repair anything in a home that can break or malfunction in a timely manner. Some of you are handy and can do much of the maintenance yourself. That's definitely a plus.

Whether you maintain the property yourself or have someone else do it, the bottom line is that you want your maintenance issues taken care of promptly. It shows your tenants that not only are you providing them someplace to stay, but also that you care about their safety and your investment. If you allow a problem to escape unresolved, you will demonstrate to your tenants that these things are of little importance.

**Something to think about

How do the rich stay rich? They keep it in the family! I have found that my most reliable contractor happens to be my cousin, Kevin. He is simply a jack-of-all-trades and has mastered a fair share of them. I rely on Kevin as needed to ensure my properties in South Carolina are taken care of. I know some people tend to trust family the least, as they perhaps could be prone to take advantage of you at the family's expense. However, I've been fortunate to not have any problems with Kevin's superior-quality work and timeliness. Thanks a million, Kevin!

Contractors. Selecting contractors is an area where you have to proceed with caution. As with any investment team, you will work with people who will make your life either a lot easier or a lot harder. If you own one property nearby and you are handy at fixing things, then you may not experience much trouble when things go awry. However, if you own multiple properties and are constantly out making deals, you should probably choose a good contractor to work for you. A good contractor can keep you in business a long time if you have developed a relationship that you can count on. They can be your eyes and ears, which leads to business longevity. They can alert you of upcoming problems long before they arise and can reduce late-night phone calls.

Because contractors are knowledgeable about many of the products and services related to property repairs, they can explain the logistics behind problems when they arise. This information will help you know in future situations whether other contractors are giving you good information. Many contractors can get deals on building materials. Contractors have more experience dealing with hardware stores than the average person. The larger stores will even have a contractor checkout line.

During peak business hours, it is probably better to allow the contractor to get any needed parts than to go yourself, as larger stores, although they offer many products, can be very short on time for customer service. I can't think of too many things more exciting than being hit with an unexpected $500 repair cost because something you've never heard of broke down, then spending two hours in a hardware store just trying to find help to buy your part and check out. This sort of thing is what you are paying the contractor to do. He won't mind going to the store for you.

Some contractors thrive off unsuspecting people who just want a job done. I would not suggest that you change your character and be mean to a contractor if that's not your nature, but contracting can be a shady business, and you want to protect yourself. Some of them can smell ignorance and connect it to money faster than you can connect smoke to fire. It never ceases to amaze me what some people will charge for labor or even parts if they suspect you to not know better. Do not look for integrity to jump out at you just because a person has a business card with two phone numbers listed on it. If you do not have anyone who comes recommended, it is a good idea to check with the Better Business Bureau (BBB) before you plunk down your hard-earned profits. You can visit the Better Business Bureau online at www.bbb.com.

Ensure that you get an estimate from the contractor and check things out to make sure he isn't overcharging you before you allow him to proceed. It is also a good idea to have him contact you if the repairs cost a certain percentage above his original quote. Some investors may allow the work to go on if the repairs don't exceed 10 percent so the contractor can continue the job without interruptions. Others may want to know if the actual cost exceeds the quoted amount by as much as a dime. This is a matter of preference. In any case, be sure to discuss money matters up front. The last thing you want is for someone to give you a bill for $500 when they told you the work was going to cost $50, tops.

Time is money, so agree on a time to get the work done. If you were promised a time of four hours to completion, then make sure that is what you get. You may want to discuss deducting fees if the work takes longer than a certain time frame.

Security deposits. I have been very fortunate in some of the renters that I have had, but dealing with some of them has not been a walk in the park. One of my tenants had a troubled relationship that she didn't disclose when we started the rental agreement. I didn't find it particularly necessary to know about her personal relationships, but that was until I found out that she and the gentleman had previous physical altercations. One evening they apparently started arguing about something, and she told him to leave. When he refused, she told him she would call the police. Eventually he left, but before long he returned, pleading with her to talk. When she refused, he tried to force his way in and kicked the door off the hinges.

This tenant did not immediately call me because it was late, but she did call me the next day and alerted me of what happened. The good thing was that she did call the police and placed a restraining order on the man. Unfortunately, she didn't have the extra money to get the door repaired. This is where her security deposit came in. I was able to call my maintenance guy, and he quickly came over the fix the broken door. I had to pay him for his service but was able to deduct the repairs from her security deposit instead of using my own money.

Security deposits work for more than broken doors. They can be your financial relief for a number of monetary issues. I have seen situations where tenants do not pay for services they used while they occupied the property. When they leave, you may find that the contractor who provided the service wants their money and your property address is all they have as a point of contact. For this reason, I recommend that you contact many of the service providers that you think your tenants may do business with during the lease.

These services may include utilities, water, premium television, telephone, and more. You should call all of these providers at such time as you and the tenant agree to cancel or end the lease. That means that you should have in your lease contract that neither the tenant nor the landlord can break the lease without some period of advance notice, perhaps thirty or sixty days.

Regardless of the timing, once you or your tenant makes it known that the contract will be terminated (or will end naturally), you should begin calling these service providers to see if there are any outstanding balances. If there are, make them known to the tenant so that they have time to either pay any outstanding balances or clarify any confusion. If they leave without taking care of these obligations, you can use their security deposit to do so. Fortunately, I have only had one outstanding bill that was presented to me after a tenant had moved on, but it is better to have the security deposit handy just in case.

Extra keys. Sometimes tenants lose keys, and they will come to you or your property management company for extras. I would recommend adding a key expense to your contract or ensuring that your security deposit will cover the cost of you having additional keys made. In addition, some renters leave in haste at the end of their leases and take the keys with them. Whether taking keys happens accidentally or not, you do not want to lose the ability to show your property to a new tenant because of something as small as a missing key to the door. For these reasons it is highly recommended that you keep extra keys to all of your properties on hand.

Non-paying tenants. This is perhaps one of the most important issues that you can face as a landlord. If a tenant pays late, you must enforce a late fee the very first time. If you don't, your tenants may get the idea that you won't do anything if they pay late, and chances are they will pay late again.

If a tenant doesn't pay his or her rent at all, I recommend that you send them friendly reminders and late notices informing them that you haven't received payment. There is a possibility that they lost track of the date and they simply forgot to send you the money when it was due.. You may want to set a reminder in your e-mail software or on your calendar to check if you have received all the rent payments that are due on that date. This way, even if a tenant forgets to send you their rent, you won't forget to ask for it.

If problems with late or unpaid rent continue, be sure to note each occurrence so you will have a record of the problem. Local laws will vary, but many will tell you that you cannot evict a tenant if they pay late until a certain number of days have passed after their rent was due. You should know the rules of engagement before you play the game so you know exactly what to do in times of trouble.

Miscellaneous problems. There are many things that can go wrong that you could not have possibly planned for. I have heard many stories of things that can go wrong with tenants. I have heard about investors putting "For Rent" signs on a renter's lawn when the renter doesn't pay on time, to give them some extra motivation to get their payment in. I have also heard where overly passionate renters have damaged property during their promiscuous escapades.

Learning about these sorts of surprises is another reason why you should read other books and articles on renters within the real estate market. As you get more involved in real estate, you will hear more and more stories. This experience will leave you better equipped to deal with problems when they arise. You have to remain attentive to how your properties are kept and what your tenants need.

Exit Strategy

You don't always have to know what you're gonna do when you get
there, but you always have to know how to get there and how to
leave.
—Willie Mickle, my father

J ust as you must study how to make wise investments and keep
good investments, you have to work diligently on how to get out
of investments. With real estate, as with any other investment,
when you decide that you have had enough—be the reason good
or bad—you must have a plan for how to exit. This is perhaps one of
the most commonly overlooked items in one's investment strategy. I
have seen quite a number of investors, myself included, overlook this
integral step.

Preparing for a sale
    When holding real estate that has appreciated greatly in value and is
still in good condition, which is what you want as an investor, you may
decide that it is time to reap the benefits of your investment by cashing
out. As I described in the chapter, "The Power of Home Equity," you
can either sell or rent out the property to acquire the cash value. You
must keep in mind that real estate is not a liquid asset, meaning you
can't turn it into cash in a few days. When markets are good, it is not
uncommon to have someone make a full offer to buy a house after it

has been on the market only a few hours. But do not think that this is the norm. Homes can take weeks, months, or even years to sell.

You will incur some costs in any real estate transaction. If you employ the services of a real estate agent, which I recommend, you will have to pay as much as 6 percent of the sales price to that agent to have the deal completed. I have seen some investors try to save a few pennies and attempt to sell the properties themselves, only to walk away with thousands less than they could have gotten. Some are knowledgeable and have done their homework but lose money on a sale anyway. A trained agent knows the market. He or she will employ appraisers to go in and find pluses and minuses that may decrease or, hopefully, increase the value of your property.

Some people think that just because the house down the street sold for one price, their house will automatically sell for the same amount, even if they have no knowledge of the other house. There may be upgrades inside the other house that have increased that house's value substantially, regardless of what meets the eye from the street. On the other hand, a home can have substantial internal damage, such as from water and drainage problems or worn-out carpet, that make the property worth much less. It is always better to have a trained appraiser give you a fair estimate.

When selling a home, you may also have to spend money to get it ready for the market. If the walls need to be touched up or the carpet needs to be cleaned, you should be prepared to spend money getting the repairs done before listing the house with an agent. A good agent will tell you what to do in your region that will make your property more appealing to potential buyers.

If your home is currently occupied by renters, you may find pluses and minuses with that situation. If there is work that needs to be done, you will have to coordinate with the occupants to schedule the work. This can add time to your sales process. In some cases, potential buyers will want to see the property multiple times and bring family and friends to see it before the purchase, creating more conflict with the current residents' schedules. Also, the tenants living at a property can add extra wear and tear to any potentially costly repairs you have just made. Ensure that you consider these things before you list your property on the market.

On the other hand, having tenants in your property while it's on the market may help you. Chances are they are knowledgeable about things in the neighborhood that even you as the owner do not know. It may be something small, such as what time the mail runs or if emergency teams have any trouble getting to the neighborhood in times of need. They can also talk about the morning rush hour and how long it may take to get to a particular area of town, right down to the minute. They will know infinitely more about the neighbors, garage sales, playground activity, and other local tidbits. All these things can really help persuade a buyer to purchase the property.

Please "bear" with us

I would certainly hope that you can come out in the black, but even the best investors sometimes have to cut their losses and walk away from a deal. The following solutions assume that the market is healthy and consumers are willing to spend. However, at the time of this writing, property owners are having a very tough time making an exit. Just as Wall Street has a bull market when times are good and a bear market when times are bad, real estate has its bull and bear markets as well.

Presently, the market has a surplus of sellers and a shortage of buyers. Owners are being offered substantially less than what they owe on their mortgages in some cases and cannot sell unless they can pay large amounts. You do not want to end up in this situation. In the automobile industry, this is commonly referred to as being "upside-down" or having negative equity. You may not be able to trade in a car because it is undervalued, and you cannot sell it without owing the lender.

These situations can be avoided by paying close attention to your investments and to the market in general. I would recommend reading national papers or watching the news regularly to stay informed. Ideally, you want to sell a property when the value is at its peak. That means you have to study the real estate business cycle to see where analysts say the market is heading. This is especially true for those who are renting property. Should the market start to head downward, you do not want to offer a two-year rental agreement thinking the market will hold strong and wait for you. If you pay attention, you can sell your property and walk away with a profit. If you fail to watch the market, you may fail to profit.

Your exit strategy should not be designed with the thought that you can wash your hands of any real estate investment in a week's time. If you spent more than a week to acquire the investment, it will commonly take at least that long to move away from it. Pay attention to the market, listen to your mentors and your team, and you can find success.

Fourth down and two to go

I'm not much of a sports fan, but I do know that in American football, a team's objective is to get to the goal line, or end zone. As long a team can advance the ball ten yards in four chances they can maintain control and continue moving toward the goal. If they can't accomplish this in three possessions, then they have to either take a long shot and go for the extra yards or punt the ball to the opposing team. The problem comes when a team is just two yards shy of the goal, fourth down and two. The objective is so close, yet so far away. It is easy to want to put it all on the line, but putting it on the line can be risky and potentially disastrous.

In real estate, just like in football, you have to have a strategy for the tough times. Sometimes success can be right at your fingertips. But when the opposition is giving you an uphill battle and has been all along, it can be foolish to forge on. If you make an unwise decision at the wrong time, it can cost you your entire investment of money, time, and other resources. You have to be smart and not greedy. Not every aspect of every investment will be a win. Don't give up on your goals and don't quit, but every now and then, you may have to punt. There is nothing inherently wrong with losing one quarter if you are willing to stay in there to win the whole game.

The Great Pyramids

Isosceles, Equilateral, and *Multi-Level*

It is important that you understand that many people's goal is to separate you from your hard-earned money. I have never been one to knock someone for what they believe will make them rich or lead them to prominence. I'm usually excited for someone if they feel they have found the way. However, I must say that there are many pyramid schemes out there that promise pie-in-the-sky dreams that just aren't worth your time.

Many people are very open and gullible to any "opportunity" that comes by. I often warn people to avoid being duped! There are get-rich-quick schemes out there on every corner, and you need not think you are exempt from getting taken even if you hold advanced degrees. From high school dropouts to Ivy League doctorates, people get taken every day. Pictures and sex sell a lot of products and services. You'd be amazed at what a few flashy documents and some hyperbole will do to make a hard-working and otherwise stubborn individual willing to part with his money.

Infomercials about investments from Wall Street to real estate air in the middle of the night and on weekends and seem to talk directly to you. You may wonder how they can know you need or want the extra money. In haste, before you know it, you have dialed the phone and ordered some fancy product kit. You sit thinking of what you will do when you begin to receive your residual income after doing little or no work. I will not name any of these specific scam organizations, but I will say that success does not come that easy. If you truly want to make it, be prepared to do lots of homework, hit some pitfalls every now and then, and spend a lot of time along the way.

Please stay conscious of people marketing stories to you saying that if you follow them to some meeting and sign up on their guest list, you will be in the company of millionaires. Let me assure you that if you want to be in the company of rich people, you can do it at Wal-Mart. There are over five million millionaires in the United States, and a large number of them shop at Wal-Mart and drive Ford F-150s. For more eye-opening facts about who really has money, I strongly recommend that you read *The Millionaire Next Door* by Thomas J. Stanley. You can also get interesting facts on wealth by visiting http://www.vonzforum. com/quotes.html.

On several different occasions, I've been invited by colleagues to their "millionaire" events. The invitation is usually given after some "lack of money" or "I'd rather be elsewhere" conversation at the water cooler, at lunch, or in the parking lot on the way home. Somehow you all end up talking about how work really sucks, and it is not the way for you. Your colleague begins to tell you about some exciting new organization that she has joined in which people are making thousands of dollars a month in their spare time. Once she sees the look of curiosity on your face, she gives you a lengthy pitch about how she has seen the light at the end of the tunnel. Shortly afterward, she talks about the person who invited her into the organization and asks if she can show you the business plan. Since the person telling you this has probably just joined, she asks if she can have some type of regional manager give you a call and answer your more detailed questions and sign you up.

Before long, this regional guy calls and begins a very similar sales pitch to the one you had with your co-worker, but he generally gives additional information that somehow leads to Ray Kroc, the founder of McDonald's. He tells how Kroc really wasn't in the hamburger business, but the franchising business. The Hamburglar conversation usually leads to the manager painting a beautiful picture in your head of you being on the beach with tons of residual income. These con artists all seem to have the same few choice phrases, such as, "We wanna get you plugged in," or, "We wanna have you on the beach in two years."

At this point either you are being nice because you like your friend, or you just haven't figured out what's going on yet and want to learn a little bit more while you totally ignore your gut feeling, which says that this is a crock of *merde*! So your friend tells you that the next exciting meeting will be some date in the near future, and that you should really attend the next one because you will have the distinct pleasure of meeting the super-duper top-dog manager who rarely comes out. This manager is normally on scene at the annual conference on some super-expensive, yet all-expenses-paid, trip to some exotic island, but you can't be a part of the conference because you haven't earned the right. So you're invited to the local meeting, and hesitantly, you go.

These events typically occur at a hotel with a host or hostess and a sign-in sheet. The individual behind the table asks you whose guest you are. You tell them your name, and if the friend who invited you isn't there yet, then you sit and wait for them while hopelessly trying to get that paper name tag to stay attached to your business suit. All the while, you observe many people such as yourself arriving with glazed-over looks on their faces that say, is this really real? Nonchalant, you continue to wait and watch as others arrive in their business attire, trying to figure out who's rich and who's not. There is a good chance you will run into someone else from work who never told you he was involved.

Before long, your friend from work arrives and begins to ask you if you have any questions or if you excited before attempting to reenergize you with the millionaire stories. She proceeds to introduce you to people who have been in the business several months longer than she has, personally. (I have yet to find anyone in these meetings who has been with the same program for several years.) So you go into the meeting room and there is a podium up front with a table to the left or right filled with some type of product that you need to sell. The first few rows of seats are empty or have been labeled "reserved." Your friend highly encourages you to sit up front so you can be more involved. Actually it is more of a tactic to get you to feel pressured not to leave after you've had enough to tell them the God-forsaken statement, "Thanks, but this is not for me."

So you sit down and the program begins. The first guest speaker is introduced as someone who was just as skeptical as you, but someone who saw the magic and moved up in the organization very rapidly.

This speaker asks the audience all types of rhetorical questions like, "Wouldn't you want to make more money in your spare time with no effort?" or, "Don't you hate your job and wouldn't you rather be elsewhere with your family?" The pep rally is enough to drive you nuts as you observe a room filled with people taking copious notes and clapping every ten minutes at some wonderful monetary figure.

After the presentation comes the forms to fill out with requests for checks and credit card numbers. You will be asked to pay a fee ranging from a few hundred dollars to a few thousand, and there is probably some type of monthly fee to go along with it. But that big payment, which you didn't really have money for in the first place, is on a credit card, so you figure you can deal with it.

At this point you have probably been at this meeting longer than you wanted to and have decided that either this program is God's new destiny for you or that you have had enough. Either way, you will get pressured to come back again or to go out and tell all your friends about the program. As you look for someone who has been involved in the program for the last few years, you just can't seem to find them. Most people stay in the program only long enough for them to figure out that this doesn't work, and then they are on to the next tunnel of hope.

As much as I hesitated to write this chapter, I felt that I had to do it. I have simply witnessed too many good people get taken by these nonsense schemes. Before you know it, such people have lost their initial investment and are making excuses for why they never got around to receiving that residual income and life on the beach.

I'm willing to bet that most people who think they want a life on the beach have yet to spend their two-week vacation sitting on the beach. I've heard quite a few people between twenty and forty talk about how they want to be retired by forty-five. My question is, to do what? Let me guess—whatever you like, right? These people want to do things like go fishing and volunteer at the homeless shelter or at local schools and churches. They can do that now if they really want to. I have met many people who have retired twice and are back at work again because they have caught every fish in the lake, mowed their grass twice, golfed thirty-six holes, and knitted three quilts in two weeks, and now they are bored out of their minds.

Your experience will be different, right? Sure it will, because you have new and improved plan for retirement, forgetting the fact that many people who live to be sixty-five will live to be eighty-five. If you retire at forty-five, that means you'll have up to forty years in retirement. That's a long time to spend on the beach.

I have seen pyramid or, as some call them, multilevel marketing schemes affect the real estate industry as well. Some make claims that the program will pay off your mortgage in as little as two or three years. They have several ways that this is supposedly done. One way asks that you take out a home equity loan or line of credit and give the schemers a fee of several thousand dollars. In return, they will pay your mortgage off for you. Others claim that through some revolutionary software, they have figured out a way to time interest rates and can tell you exactly when to make payments that will give you a lower interest rate, thereby decreasing your payment.

Please think with me for a moment. If you have lived in your current residence for five to ten years and haven't paid it off, do you really think someone else is going to do it for you in less time? I mean, is this really making sense? Mortgages have been around a long time, and you *can* pay them off. It only requires two things—lots of time, lots of money, or both. You can cut approximately nine years off your mortgage just by making one extra payment a year. If you don't have the entire extra payment in one lump sum, just break it up into twelve payments and add that amount to your monthly mortgage payment. The results will be the same. Observe the balance line of the chart below of someone making just the required monthly payment each month and you will see that after 21 years they still have a \$52842.20 balance. If they added only $1/12^{th}$ of their mortgage payment in addition to their regular monthly payment they will be finished paying off the mortgage in 21 years eliminating thousands in interest charges.

	First Month of Year 1	5 years Later	10 years later	20 years later	21 years later
Mortgage Amount	100000	100000	100000	100000	100000
Mortgage Term	30 years	30 years	30 years	30 years	30 years
Interest Rate	7%	7%	7%	7%	7%
Start Date	4/6/2008	4/6/2008	4/6/2008	4/6/2008	4/6/2008
Monthly Pmt	665.3	665.3	665.3	665.3	665.3
Month/Year	5/6/2008	2013	2018	2028	2029
Payment	665.3	665.3	665.3	665.3	665.3
Principal Paid	81.97	116.2	164.73	331.05	354.98
Interest	583.33	549.1	500.57	334.25	310.32
Total Interest		34598.84	66149.26	117306.9	121164
Balance	99918.03	94015.39	85647.65	56969.03	52842.2
add 1/12th monthly payment	92	92	92	92	
New Payment	757.3	757.3	757.3	757.3	671.49
Principal Paid	173.97	246.62	349.62	702.62	667.6
Interest Paid		510.68	407.68	54.69	3.89
Interest	583.33	33493.87	61172.56	91182.11	91511.72
Balance	99826.03	87298.42	69538.96	8672.21	0

To see an example with your own mortgage please visit www.fastfind.com.

What did that little bit of insight cost you? Just the price of this book. You didn't have to sign up for anybody's program. You were not asked for your credit card number. I didn't require a $3,000 fee. That is as simple as it can be. However, if you just want to contribute to my Lamborghini Murcielago fund, by all means, send me an e-mail, and I'll provide further instructions.

Review

"The Essence of Leadership"

A true leader has the confidence to stand alone, the courage to make tough decisions, and the compassion to listen to the needs of others. He does not set out to be a leader, but becomes one by the quality of his actions and the integrity of his intent. In the end, leaders are much like eagles ... they don't flock, you find them one at a time.
—Successories, a motivational products store

I hope that while reading this book you have gained new insight into the many preliminary steps involved in making real estate investments. If I have done my job, you should walk away from this book with a clearer picture of the process than before. As you go out and begin to give a more intelligent look at the residential real estate world, I hope that you will realize that it starts with a much wider view than simply on an individual property. For those of you who have already begun investing, I hope that I have provided you with another angle or a better approach to the things that you have already been doing.

You are about to connect or reconnect with the opportunity to gain wealth, but please keep your excitement contained as not every investment is a good investment. Keep in mind all the overnight success stories and get-rich-quick schemes that are waiting like traps to take your money. Many successful people have said it takes *years* to become an overnight success. Stay mindful of where the market is in terms of troughs and crests so that you can avoid buying too high and having to sell or attempt to sell to low. Use your home equity wisely to make investments and try to avoid using your equity to purchase things that will create additional liabilities that you won't be able to reap any monetary rewards from later.

Ensure that you create the right legal entities so that you can properly protect your assets. Make good use of the services of good legal council and CPAs to help you magnify the benefits of investing. Take full advantage of business write-offs so that you pay the least amount of taxes necessary. Become familiar with all your business entity options so that you can change your entity if one proves to be more beneficial than the other. In other words, if you begin to acquire a lot of properties as an LLC, maybe you will be better off switching entities and becoming a corporation. Do the research and find out what fits your situation best.

Successful investing is a process that will be repeated over time. Don't go it alone—engage the skills of a good team. It is much better to listen to someone who has gone before you and made mistakes so that you can avoid them. Try to engage your mentors and team members on investment decisions early in your research process. During your research phase, remember that houses reside in communities, communities in counties, and counties in states. Be sure that you research many angles before you spend money by checking out the various elements that will come with your property, such as the community, homeowner's association, neighbors, and mortgages. Information from county government offices can have a significant impact on your investment. The county wants you to succeed just as much as you do.

When looking to acquire new properties, be sure to make as many notes as possible about all the properties that you are considering while you are in front of them. It is difficult to remember exactly what details were involved for each property, even though at the time you are sure you will remember them later. Don't underestimate the power of pictures, not only for motivation for something you want, but also for the details of something you need. Using a digital camera allows you to store a substantial amount of pictures on a minimal-size piece of hardware.

When dealing with tenants, keep your business in perspective. There will be challenges and there may be conflicts, but you have the ability to mitigate risks and problems by implementing the proper checks of tenants' history. Make careful decisions and plan an appropriate exit strategy. If you fail to plan, then you plan to fail. Stay aware of trends that affect your investments by reading periodicals and conversing with other investors.

Move carefully and stay mindful that making money from investments is a journey and not a destination. Just as you will have fun and prosperous seasons, you will also have difficult ones. Stay in the there and be thankful that eventually seasons change.

Don't Ever Give Up

"Be encouraged no matter what's going on …"
—Lyrics from the gospel song *Be Encouraged*, by Fred Hammond and
Kirk Franklin

As I stated before, to gain wealth in something, you have to do
something well over and over again. This is why you need a
process. Even with a process, you can run into tough times. I
urge you to not let the tough times get you down. You simply have to
keep fighting and protecting your dream. The introductory chapter to
this book talked about how I turned around my loss of an $80,000-a-
year job with one that paid only eight dollars an hour. That was just
one example of a tough time I was thankful for.

I recently had a conversation with a young lady named Ms.
Madstam. She was convinced that she was going through a really tough
time in her life, and I'm sure she was. As she looked for answers, I told
her to turn to the Creator, the Alpha and the Omega, the Doctor who
never lost a patient, and the Lawyer who never lost a case. It's not like
she didn't know about God or lacked spirituality, but like some when
it gets tough, she began to question God and asked why he was doing
this to her. I understood how she felt—it seemed like God the Supreme
Being was so far away, and she needed earthly answers. I encouraged

her to listen to the first twelve minutes of the *Steve Harvey Morning Show*.

Mr. Harvey is a well-known comedian who is not necessarily known for clean language. However, he had a strong mother who was strong believer, so although he may have said a number of derogatory things on stage, he never forgets where his blessings come from. Therefore, he began his show each day with real talk for the soul. I believed it was there that Ms. Madstam could find some of the earthly answers she was searching for.

I think she believed that because it seemed like my life was going so well, I had things all figured out. Regardless of how things looked, I assured her things were not always as they seemed. My success did not just start one day and continue to grow without any challenges. In fact, it was the challenges that really grabbed my attention and led me to success. I'd like to share with you a few more examples to let you know turnarounds are not just one-time things.

Well before I lost my comfortable job in information technology, I faced other challenges in college. The Citadel is a unique college experience. It is a campus that is set behind walls that cadets cannot freely enter and exit. Its many restrictions are designed to create a number of things including camaraderie, leadership, and discipline. Financially, the school can be just as restrictive. It is not unusual for students at traditional colleges to have local part-time or even full-time jobs while attending class. The Citadel does not allow this. There are only a few part-time work-study jobs available, and these have very limited hours. If your parents are wealthy, it is not a big deal, but if your family finances are insufficient, then the lack of freedom can lead to very difficult financial times. The benefit of a closed campus was that because students were not allowed to roam the streets freely, they could not rack up tons of junk debt.

I was fortunate because I could join the Army National Guard to help offset some of my expenses. I was able to purchase a reliable used car, and I obtained two credit cards. I was very responsible with my finances and had an occasional $200 to splurge with every now and then. I remained within my financial limits for the most part, as my credit limits were only $1,000 and $2,500. Therefore, I could only do so much damage.

Because weekend-duty guard drill was only required once a month, I sometimes ran out of money before I ran out of month. During my junior year, I was finally able to get a campus job and could more easily offset my weekend expenses. For my entire junior year, life was good.

I had two sources of income and few monthly expenses outside of student loans, which were deferred until six months after graduation.

I went home for the summer and eagerly anticipated my final year of college. When I returned I was hit with a very rude awakening. I went into the Citadel's campus police department to find that my part-time job was now filled by a full-time police officer and my services were no longer needed. I immediately asked, "What am I supposed to do about my bills?" The police officer said maybe there were some other campus work-study jobs available. I knew that wouldn't work because those few jobs had been taken by the guys who had had them last year. I just knew I was doomed, because with only one job my expenses would exceed my monthly Army income.

Before long, the late notices began to come in the mail, and I felt absolutely horrible about where my finances were heading. I didn't know what a credit report or credit score was, but I knew that if you didn't pay your bills on time things would not be good for your personal finances. As the year went on, I got further and further behind on my credit card bills. I felt if I could just hang on until graduation, just two or three months of a full-time job would clear my delinquent balances. But even though I had three solid job offers lined up, I decided instead to go to Harvard University to study Ukrainian.

I believed that all I had to do was get a part-time job somewhere in the area to help me survive while I attended classes. Unfortunately for me, the area I lived in wasn't particularly welcoming to black people. I distinctly remember going into several businesses with help wanted signs hanging on the door only to enter and receive a cold look of disgust. Business owners couldn't even believe I had the nerve to enter their establishments. In the meantime, my debts were still not being paid off. Before long, I left Harvard and began working.

By this time, I had nearly lost my car. All of my credit cards bills were now with collection agencies, and I had to receive the rude, nasty phone calls of a low-paid, uneducated customer service agent who somehow believed he had dominion over me. It was a humiliating experience. I recall saying, "God, why is all this happening to me?" What I didn't realize was that the biggest blessing of my next few years was being orchestrated right in the midst of all this.

As I began my first technology job, I had a one-track mind—to get rid of all my outstanding obligations so I could get a fresh start. That is exactly what I did. Since I had no credit cards, I couldn't charge anything, so all my purchases were bought with cash or layaway.

I recall sitting in my good friend Charnita's office talking with some other fresh college graduates. Somehow we got on the subject of renting apartments, buying houses, and monthly debt. They all began to talk about the thousands of dollars they had in credit card debt and how it would keep them from owning their first townhomes. As they went around the room, all I could hear was, "I have four thousand dollars," "I have six thousand dollars," "That's nothing. I have ten thousand dollars."

Then they turned to me. I said, "I don't have any credit card debt." They were all flabbergasted. They felt I was somehow smarter than the rest of them and had the ability to turn away from all those illustrious worldly goods. They couldn't have been more wrong, actually. It wasn't my doing. I believe God shook my life up during senior year to prepare me for what was to come. Because I didn't have any credit card debt, I was able to bypass the apartment rental stage of life, and my first residence was my own.

It was with that first purchase that I was able to secure a home in the DC area before the nearly unreachable prices set in. Today, while my colleagues live in nice homes and townhomes, I live in a $1.5 million mansion. I assure you it had less to do with my conventional way of doing things, because if it were left up to me, I assure you I would have been out there buying those nice, material things, just like everybody else.

Another example of a drastic turnaround in my life occurred several years later. I began paying close attention to the stock market around 1999, when the United States was fully engaged in a bull market. All the dot-com stocks were growing like nothing ever seen before. Companies were launching unprecedented returns and it looked like the rise would continue indefinitely. Because I worked in the technical arena, I was sure I understood technology companies like Microsoft, Cisco, and Charter Communications, just to name a few.

I watched stocks rise, and everyone in my office felt the excitement of Wall Street. Young people talked of new cars and new houses and lives of prosperity. I knew for sure that I was going to ride the wave with them. I began buying stocks as well. I figured that as long as I paid attention to the news and read magazines such as *Fortune* and *Newsweek* and simply purchased their top picks, then surely I would be just fine. I began spending all of my extra income on technology stocks.

Before long, things started to change. The record high stock prices began to taper off. The buzz was starting to quiet down. In the meantime, there were many analysts still saying to hang in there and that things would get better. I believed them, like so many other young, naïve investors. Days without the expected returns turned into weeks, and weeks turned into months. Hefty brokerage account balances began to dwindle. As my account was suddenly cut in half, I realized I had to sell or risk losing everything. So there I was, once again thinking, "God, why me?" How could all that reading of the magazines and all the watching of CNNFN just go to waste? All of my little stock dreams began to fade. Once again, I was in a storm.

At that point I realized that maybe I wasn't as smart as I thought I was. I began to research more about the stock market. I began learning things, such as Wall Street was one of the most well-known yet least understood streets in the world. Here was a marketplace that was over four hundred years old that had once been a wall of mud and brush to keep the cows in and the Indians out.

I began to study concepts such as market caps, P/E ratios, liquidity, and insider trading. I became familiar with the time value of money, dollar-cost averaging, and indexing. I learned why the S&P 500 was called what it was, as with the Wilshire 5000. I began studying bonds in addition to stocks and learned of more complex investments such as private equity and hedge funds.

I was able to entertain conversations about Wall Street with a degree of intelligence when I ran into a very motivating young millionaire named Mark Spradley, who told me the story of how the field of private equity, or buying and selling businesses through complex valuation techniques and business relationships, allowed him to walk into the bank with personal checks for millions of dollars and no real sense of urgency to cash them. He could simply walk in, make an unusually large deposit or withdrawal, and continue his day as if nothing out of the ordinary ever happened. Thanks to my introduction to Mark, I went back to school again, at Keller Graduate School, to hone my valuation techniques and to take a serious look into this field. A owe you a ton of gratitude, Mr. Spradley.

I gained a renewed strength and understanding of complex financial investments. Before long I was able to read the daily papers and understand what they meant when they used Wall Street terms. My colleagues again thought I was some kind of savant who somehow instinctively knew more than they did. They began to listen intently to the things I was saying and trusting me more than others. I gained enough insight to realize I needed more. With the knowledge I did have, I was able to get into Georgetown's Certified Financial Planning program. There I learned infinitely more than I ever thought there was to know. While there, I was able to gain a scholarship to continue my studies.

I have to say here again that this turnaround was not my doing. As much as I'd like to say one good thing led to another, it was quite the contrary. Things have never come easy for me. I had to endure yet another hardship, only to realize that after the storm was over, it was really a blessing in disguise. I do not like going through hardships any more than anyone else; however, I have come to realize that God places us in these trying times to strengthen us and show us better things that life offers.

I can give other examples, but I think you get the point. As you get out there and make your investments, please remember that if you experience turbulence, move very cautiously and observe as much as you can because something has been sent to grab your attention. I assure you, not giving up and mustering up the strength to go on will make you a much better investor. For some of the most amazing stories of how our most well-known companies made it, I recommend an international best seller called *100 Great Businesses* by Emily Ross and Angus Holland. The book features stories of the early years of companies such as Pixar, Amazon, The Kellogg company, Porsche, Starbucks, and many others.

I want to share with you two final stories that focus on perseverance and the benefits that await you if you can just weather the storm. I recall reading a story from a book about Donald Trump's comeback in which he talked about one of the lowest points in his life. His company was billions of dollars in debt with a lot of it he was personally responsible for. He talked about how the markets crashed, and many things outside of his control came down on him. At three o'clock one night he was summoned to the boardroom to discuss a complex business strategy and where he would have to account for his financial woes. It was a rainy winter night in New York City. He had to walk several blocks, and by the time he arrived at the office, he was soaked.

I won't go into all the details, but I recommend that you read *Trump: The Art of the Comeback*. At this low point, instead of going into the meeting with his head in his hands, he entered with the thought of thriving and making a remarkable comeback, even though he deemed this time the toughest of his career. To have this type of mindset at that hour takes a tremendous amount of courage, commitment, and belief in oneself.

Trump has been called glitzy and glittery, but one thing is for sure—he doesn't believe in giving up, even during the tough times. I know all too well the mindset one has to have to persevere through the storm. In addition, I can give a very vivid image of what can happen when life gives you these types of situations. Coal and diamonds are two precious commodities that both require great pressures from the earth to form. You can decide if you are going to use your experience to become a charred piece of coal or to come out of your pressure cooker shining like a five-carat diamond. Unlike coal and diamonds, which do not have any choice on which path they will take, you do. Which will you decide? Are you going to be a piece of coal or a clear-cut diamond? You will have pressure either way.

During December 2007, my girlfriend Crystal and I decided to take a casual trip through Northern Virginia wine country. I wanted to show her a quaint, yet wealthy, little town called Middleburg. We drove slowly and casually through the small town observing its unique boutiques, shops, and particularly the soon-to-come high-end resort and spa that would be built by business mogul and BET co-founder Sheila Johnson.

As we left the town and headed back toward Washington, I observed a model home that was built by Elite Builders of Northern Virginia. I had seen the model several times as they were constructing it. It was a very nice estate home nestled on several acres of land. We went inside and observed this model and all of its nice features. We were greeted by a friendly sales agent named Christine who said she would answer any questions we had while there. I wasn't yet familiar with this builder, but I felt they paid attention to the small details that can really make a house—details such as the right selection of cabinets in a gourmet kitchen or decorative iron rails to show off a marvelous staircase. I couldn't help hearing the sounds of the smooth jazz coming from the speakers on the flat-screen television in the living room. Once I stopped to take notice, I realized that the jazz was being played on a DVD showcasing a much larger, more beautiful home.

I asked Christine where the home on the DVD was located. She informed me that this was the owner's new residence, but he would be glad to sell it if someone was willing to pony up the twelve-million-dollar price tag. I quickly thanked her for sharing the information but was very forward in letting her know that I wasn't quite at that level yet. However, I did enjoy seeing the home. All of the details that were in the model we were seeing were displayed to an even greater level in this house on the DVD. I knew without question that the home on the

DVD was far superior to any home I had seen to date, including the ones in Potomac. I'm certain the element of the home that interested me the most was its towering height.

I live in an estate home with ten-foot ceilings on the first floor and nine-foot ceilings on the second floor, and while mine is far from short, I have seen that some homes appear substantially taller. I studied this as I viewed the model homes, but between getting answers to my inquiries on maximum height standards in building codes and regulations of measurements from ground to roof, it was about as clear as mud as to how someone could build a house that tall. Either way, I was still interested and felt that to truly declare a house a mansion, it needed the towering height that was clearly on display in this house. We continued to view the model while making small talk with Christine and another couple who had recently purchased, and then we were on our way. As we were leaving, I asked Christine if I could have a copy of the DVD, and she obliged.

Roughly ten days passed before I decided to watch the video again. I didn't feel much like watching it because I was weathering a tough season. In spite of the several great years I had had with my real estate investments, this year was consistently dealing me punishing blows. I had not seen the downturn coming and had certainly not anticipated that it would be as bad as it was. It was a Wednesday night after I had had a fairly long day before I retreated down to my theatre to plop the video in.

Once the images were up on the big screen and the smooth music was radiating out of the speakers, the mansion was just as I remembered. It was handsome, stately, and majestic all at the same time. I decided that night that I had to see this house in real life; a collage of vivid images simply wasn't enough. By Friday, I had had a few more days of not-so-good news. I found that I was facing a fifty-thousand-dollar pay cut, one of my mortgage companies had gone belly up, and my parents were facing some unexpected financial hurdles. I thought, God help me!

I planned a trip to visit with my parents knowing that the following days had the potential to get even tougher, so I decided that before I headed south I needed to see something positive. I knew then that I wasn't going to drive one mile south without seeing the twelve-million-dollar house to gain some inspiration, the inspiration to tell me that I had to stay the course if I eventually wanted the level of success that I desired. Without another thought I called Christine and told her of my desire. She again mentioned that if I was to see the inside of the house I would have to show proof that I qualified for the twelve-million-dollar price tag. I told her that I did not need to see the inside of the house and the outside would be just fine. She understood, and gave me the address and directions.

I quickly gathered my tripod and digital camera and headed toward Great Falls, where the mansion was located. I had driven through the area before and seen the very upscale homes that this community offered. As I turned onto the street where the house was located, I decided to set aside my directions and let my eyes be my guide. It wasn't long before I saw it, and boy did I see it. It was more magnificent than any picture on a DVD could ever display it. With its soaring height and massive presence, it towered over any other house on the street, like a gargoyle standing next to a midget. I slowly pulled up to the mansion and just stared for a moment. I was aware that the owner was occupying the residence but decided that I had to have a picture of this masterpiece.

I got out of my vehicle and began to set up my tripod and camera without any hesitation. I finally got the majority of the property in view and I was ready to press the shutter button. As I applied pressure to my index finger, steadying my camera, I suddenly heard a voice saying, "Hey! What are you doing?" Startled, I began to yell back that I recently visited the model near Middleburg and was given this location by the sales agent. When the gentleman asked me who the sales agent was, I responded, "Christine." He gestured for me to come on up.

I wasn't quite sure what to expect as I stood there waiting for the iron gates to open, but whatever it was, I felt was it would put me closer to the house than I had ever expected. As I finally made my way up the hill, I found that the voice belonged to the owner, Mr. Irfan Totonji. He was accompanied by his lovely wife and two children. He asked me to explain further about why I had come, and I obliged. He told me that since I was there he would allow me to see the entry foyer, but he appreciated if I didn't take any pictures. I quickly assured him that not only had I not taken any, but that I would respect his wishes.

Irfan and I entered through the wood, hand-carved, imported double doors in the front while his wife and children used a side entrance. He opened the door, I walked in, and my mouth just dropped. The entry foyer was a Middle Eastern work of art. It was an absolute masterpiece with its tall columns, the tops of which were hand carved and seemingly made with gold. The shiny marble heated floors reflected the hand-painted dome that towered sixteen feet above me. I was quite sure the expression on my face must have said this was all I imagined, and then some. After I regrouped, I noticed that Irfan's wife and kids had now joined us in the foyer.

As I looked around, I asked him who had decorated this place. He said, "My wife." I turned to her and said, "Really?" She kindly nodded, and then invited me to the rear of the house to showcase some of her other interior decorating talents. By now I think the family had realized I meant no harm, and we gleefully began to tour this work of art. The son wanted to show me the movie theatre with its fully reclining leather seats, while the daughter wanted to show me the fully customized elevator that serviced all three levels. Irfan would go on to show me the office before his wife showcased her favorite room of the house, the kitchen. It was easily one of the largest kitchens I'd ever seen, with two islands, a six-burner gas range, and a butler's pantry that looked like something from a five-star hotel. The room came complete with a crystal chandelier and heated marble floors.

Soon after, this God-loving and warm family allowed me to join them at the table for juice, cheesecake, and cappuccino served in what appeared to be solid gold china. Then we visited the basement level and I came across a room that I had never seen before, a prayer room. I thought to myself that this was interesting. They told me that they prayed a lot and that they were very thankful for the blessings they had. It was there that they explained to me that all the Arabic writing found in paintings and in the dome was very biblical and expressed how they loved God and how to them, God was everything. In fact, the mansion was named Iman Manor after Irfan's daughter, as Iman means "faith."

As we stood there in that room, I had to confess to them that I had really needed to see this house today, and how my week and year were going much less than desirably. With a heart of concern they began to ask how they could help, inquiring about what they could do. I simply told them I wasn't sure at this point, but they let me know that they would pray for me and my family. As far as I was concerned, just letting me view the entry foyer was ten times more than I could have expected.

After we spent some time observing the five-hundred-CD changer, the pool, and the birdhouse, we found ourselves back in the kitchen engaging in delightful conversation. It was there that Irfan's wife asked me if I was married. I told her I wasn't but that I had a delightful girlfriend and that we were definitely looking to get married. What she said next was about as jaw-dropping as the entry foyer. She said, "Why don't you get married here?" I thought, oh my gosh! Is she serious? She was offering her twenty-thousand-square-foot, twelve-million-dollar house for my wedding ceremony. Not only was she serious, the entire family was. I was in absolute disbelief. We continued to chat for about an hour and a half, at which time I told them I had to be on my way. As I prepared myself to leave, the family gave me a rack of lamb and rice to take with me on the journey down south and threw in an autographed picture of one of their famous NBA friends as a gift.

As I think back on this story, it sounds absolutely unbelievable. I assure you that I couldn't have made it up if I wanted to. I think it is a true testimony to so many things. First and foremost, I believe that anyone who questions the existence of God should immediately be made whole, as this was about as much divine intervention as anyone could have gotten, showing that He has the power to intervene and make impossible things happen. Second, I believe it clearly displays what Donald Trump has said many times, which is to never, ever quit. Never give up on your dreams. Once again, Trump was right, and this was a real estate story that proved that adage to the fullest. The truth is short-lived, but a well-told lie is immortal. I sincerely hope that this story stands for a very, very long time. Trouble doesn't last forever.

Pictured below is the work of art called Iman Manor. I titled this picture Von's Blind Iman, which means "Von's Blind Faith." How else could all of this have happened without me listening to the little voice in my head that said to go ahead and drive forty-five miles out of my way to I find something worthy of investing my time?

Now that you have taken the most important step in investing by doing some research, if you want to see if you are financially healthy enough to invest, please have a glance at the case study on www.vonzforum. com/book.html. After giving a year to the study of financial planning, it would be very irresponsible of me to not have you evaluate your own financial house before you invest in the house of someone else. Keep me posted on your progress. You can e-mail me at vonzforum@cs.com, as I'd love to hear how you are doing along the way.

Suggested Additional Reading

Here is a list of books that I have read that have given me insight into real estate investing that I feel is worth sharing. They are in no order of importance, and no one book weighs any heavier than the other. They are all great, and I recommend reading them all. You should become an avid reader of real estate investment books to gain a very broad knowledge of other successful peoples' experiences. You can find many of these books in the business section of your favorite book stores.

The Millionaire Next Door: The Surprising Secrets of America's Wealthy. Thomas J. Stanley and William D. Danko. Fine Communications, 2002

There is a gut-wrenching difference between high income and wealth. Just because someone makes $100,000 a year doesn't make them wealthy anymore than someone who earns $30,000 a year doesn't make them poor. The rich measure their money by net worth and not income. This book is a detailed illustration from two PhD's who studied the affluent class for over twenty years to highlight the difference between those who *look* wealthy and those who *are* wealthy. This is by far one of the best books I've ever read to help determine why I wasn't rich when I thought I was.

Millionaire Republican: Why Rich Republicans Get Rich—and How You Can Too! Wayne A. Root. Penguin Group, 2006.

Root's book takes a strong stab at the record selling *Rich Dad, Poor Dad* for not recognizing that the rich dad was probably a Republican and took a much more capitalistic view to money, wealth and power than the poor dad who was probably a democrat and took a more traditional or conventional look at gaining wealth getting a good education and working for a good company for many years in hopes of retiring rich. While there is nothing wrong with either way, Root really points out that party lines can make a significant difference in wealth. This book was also a classic example of while you may start out reading a book to learn about one person; you can find significant jewels of information about another. It was here that I learned where Bill Gates met Paul Allen and how their early success was almost destined from their days at Lakeside, the most prestigious and expensive private school in the Pacific Northwest. I also learned here that Donald Trump was dealt a "Trump" card long before he became known as *The Donald*!

Mortgage Confidential: What You Need to Know That Your Lender Won't Tell You. David Reed. AMACOM, 2006.

On the very simplest level I finally realized that Fannie Mae was a nickname for Federal National Mortgage Association and Freddie Mac was a name given to the Federal Home Loan Mortgage Corporation. On a very detailed level, I learned that the chances of a mortgage loan being approved by a group of people overlooking your application are not likely. Instead, your loan is sent through a computer program called the AUS (automated underwriting system). I also found out that underwriters are not checking for assets and debt ratios but simply verifying that the information needed is present in the loan file. Perhaps this is what caused a lot of the 2007 mortgage melt-down. As an investor, your most important key to acquiring property is the mortgage and you want to understand what is really happening behind the scenes once you submit your paperwork. If you don't, chances are a savvy lender can fill your loan with ridiculous fees and congratulate you on your approval meanwhile your excitement and contentment will make you the laughing stock of the lender's office because you just got duped!

100 Great Businesses and the Minds Behind Them. Emily Ross and Angus Holland. Sourcebooks, Incorporated, 2005.

This book tells many stories of how the most admired companies and branded images got their starts many times on shoestring budgets. The reason they made it is largely due to their willingness to keep on moving despite life's adversity. Oprah Winfrey and Sean "Puff"

Combs just to name a few are some of the wealthiest and most well-known celebrities that world know but their lives didn't start off very celebrated at all. Oprah was sexually abused by her family members during her early years and had to mentally tolerate having a baby at age fourteen, who died shortly after birth. Today she is the reigning queen of television and has a net worth of over a billion dollars. Puffy was raised by a single mom on the tough streets of New York after his father was killed in a drug related incident while he was just two years old. After a brief stint at Howard University, he accepted a role as an unpaid intern at Uptown Records. Refusing to accept anything less than lifestyles of the rich and "ghetto fabulous", he made a name for himself in the urban community as a prodigy child for remixing records. Today he is living a dream with the success he has created with his Bad Boy entertainment group which includes a restaurant chain, movie production and an advertising company.

The Peebles Principles: Tales and Tactics from an Entrepreneur's Life of Winning Deals, Succeeding in Business, and Creating a Fortune from Scratch. Donahue R. Peebles, and J.P. Faber. Wiley, John & Sons, Incorporated, 2007.

R. Donahue Peebles is currently a multi-billion dollar developer with a personal net worth in excess of $500 million. Of all the books I have read about the power of using other people's money, he has probably prospered off this concept the most. In his book, *The Peebles Principles,* he talks about the first property that he acquired in his early twenties, although, it was a large commercial office building, it provided him a yearly income of several hundred thousand dollars which made him a multi-millionaire overnight. From that point on, he has steadily climbed the ladder of success. After completing a number of projects in Washington, DC, Mr. Peebles re-located to South Florida where he developed Miami Beach's prestigious Residences at The Bath Club, his only residential project to date. Although some residential projects are not significant revenue producers, Mr. Peebles performed his due diligence and was able to create and capitalize on one of Miami Beach's signature developments. Just as his book outlines the value of research and leaving no small detail to chance, Mr. Peebles understands the power of maintaining strong political ties and hosts fundraisers for the political elite from local representatives all the way to the presidential level.

Real Estate Riches: How to Become Rich Using Your Banker's Money. Dr. Dolf de Roos. Wiley, John & Sons, Incorporated, 2004.

Dr. de Roos ousted the conventional "go to school, get an education and get a get job" way of life long before he even graduated from high school. His parents, like many, have been taught to believe a good education is the key to financial success and while it certainly can be, education is no guarantee for monetary success. He isn't saying that you should not have a good education and you should but he knows it is not a guarantee. After spending some time thinking about how his parents believe that education equates to money, he thought if that were the case then college professors should be the richest people around which is certainly not the case. Dr. de Roos purchased his first property while he was still a teenager and made a profit while he was still a student. From that point on he continued his studies as an engineer all the way to the PhD level but he took notice of the value in real estate investing. He is one of the few self-made millionaires who can lay claim to the fact of never having a job.

Rich Dad, Poor Dad: What the Rich Teach Their Kids About Money--That the Poor and Middle Class Do Not! Robert T. Kiyosaki and Sharon L. Lechter. Grand Central Publishing, 1998.

This book will remain on the New York Times Bestseller's list for many years to come because of the way Kiyosaki describes his two dads'. Although the educated dad held several advanced degrees he was always going to live a life from check to check while the dad without a formal education was going to live a very prosperous life and would never rely on a check from an employer. I gained a very different understanding about the difference between assets and liabilities. In the midst of the story of the varying rich dad and poor dad lifestyles, you are able to pick up that Kiyosaki is an avid real estate investor and have made millions through his investment properties.

The Richest Man Who Ever Lived: King Solomon's Secrets to Success, Wealth, and Happiness. Steven K. Scott. Doubleday Publishing, 2006.

King Solomon is believed to be the richest man who ever lived, even more so than John D. Rockefeller. Estimates today would suggest that he would have been a "trillionaire". The author of this book has attained riches by adhering to the same words of wisdom that King Solomon lived by taken from the biblical Book of Proverbs. I, just as many other wealthy people believe that a spiritual life is essential to attaining money. Proverbs 28:19 states, "Without a vision, the people perish." You have to have a vision for what you want out of life whether you obtain the vision through taking pictures or writing definitive goals. Proverbs 23:7 states, "As a man thinks in his heart, so is he." If you feel you will be successful at investing that is exactly what you will be.

Secrets of the Millionaire Mind: Mastering the Inner Game of Wealth. Harv T. Eker. Collins, 2005.

I refer to this book a lot because it is saturated with motivational one-liners that make the absolute best sense. Here are a few examples: "Don't wait to buy real estate, buy real estate and wait." How much does the place you live in today cost compared to how much it cost fifty years ago? If you buy it now and hold on the value will certainly go up.

"Did you know that most people earn within 20 percent of their closest friends?" It only took a few Investment Forums for me to confirm this.

"Expenses will always rise in direct proportion to income." Once I began to study my personal financial situation, I realized that the occasional raise and bonus was only going to make me a slightly more in-debt slave. We generally want we don't have and what we don't have always costs just a little more.

The Secret. Rhonda Byrne. Simon & Schuster Adult Publishing Group, 2006.

Being rich is a mentality but so is being poor. What many people don't realize is they speak things into existence. If you continuously talk about having a prosperous day that is exactly what you will have because you tune your minds to it. At the same time, people who talk about how miserable life is will always have a miserable life based on the same reason. The writers of this book feel that the Secret is not only words they live by but also a way of life. Oprah Winfrey believes the secret is one of the reasons she is where she is today. The secret that they talk about is the law of attraction and this book highlights many examples of people being attracted to the things their minds focus on the most. I am a firm believer in this book and its principles.

Trump: Think Like a Billionaire: Everything You Need to Know About Success, Real Estate, and Life. Donald J. Trump, and Meredith Mciver. Random House, 2004.

Trump: The Art of the Comeback. Donald J. Trump and Kate Bohner. Random House, Incorporated, 1997.

Trump University Asset Protection 101. J.J. Childers. Wiley, John & Sons, Incorporated, 2007.

The Wealth Builder's Blueprint. Donald J. Trump. Trump University Press, 2006.

Donald Trump lives a lifestyle that so many of us dream of. From his billion dollar empire to his hit television show, everywhere he goes he commands a lot of attention. While not everyone likes his flashy lifestyle, only few can argue that he is at least willing to show people how it's done. Trump has not only written many best-selling books that give straight talk on how he has master-minded many business deals but he also has created Trump University to give even more lessons to create real estate wealth. I like all of Trumps books because the chapters are short allowing you to read one or two during quick breaks. It was in his book *Trump: Think Like a Billionaire: Everything You Need to Know About Success* that I began to read passionately about many business books as he mentioned you have to read all the best sellers to stay abreast on what's going on. He also remains an avid reader himself and recommends reading the great newspapers daily. It was because of his instruction that I began to read the Washington Post business section everyday to keep me abreast of new developments, events and happenings where many successful business people congregate. Simply reading those eight or nine pages has placed me in the company of many successful people. Trump caps his instruction with *Trump University Asset Protection 101* where he teams with J.J. Childers to explain in great detail what needs to happen to keep all the properties you accumulate. Whether you agree with his lifestyle or not is for you to decide but I have not found many other billionaires who are willing to give you an hour by hour typical day in their life breakdown.

About The Investment Forum
"Essence of Imagination"

What we can easily see is only a small portion of what is possible.
Imagination is having the vision to see what is just below the surface,
to picture what is essential, but invisible to the eye.
—Successories, a motivational products store

The Investment Forum started in October of 2004 with the goal of sharing investment information. Its mission is to provide substantial, substantive, and pragmatic investment knowledge on topics such as personal financial planning, real estate, securities, and other business ventures. This knowledge is provided through real-life experiences with the aim to better educate those who desire to become better stewards of their finances. The result is to create options for the future.

The Investment Forum looks to build financial leaders who can change the course of a family's financial legacy and create generational wealth. The power of what one person can provide for a family's financial legacy may have a domino effect for generations to come. We want our members to be armed with foresight and insight to stop unproductive behavior and inappropriate spending. In addition, we want to educate our members and correct their mistakes so that they set good examples.

The first forum contained thirty people, but today, the group has over one hundred members, three of whom sit on the board. The forums have catered to everyone from curious first-time homeowners to mutual fund investors. It has also captured knowledge and insight from world-renowned business leaders and high-ranking politicians.

Because we share experiences, we learn key steps for success that include not only what to do, but also what not to do. We look to ensure people are financially healthy before they make investments by asking tough questions about what their plans are if their investments do not work out. We believe making money in investments is important, but not losing money can be equally important.

In our quest to educate, we share books, CDs, and seminars that we have found helpful along the way. A large percentage of the members are looking for the same thing: to become financially healthy first and then independently wealthy, although they go about gaining those objectives in different ways. We believe wealth can be obtained through years of solid investments while not being sidetracked through frivolous spending and get-rich-quick schemes.

We believe in the power of strong social networks and understand that greatness yields greatness. Therefore, we stay involved in our community with new projects that provide opportunities for good returns on our investments. We believe there is strength in numbers, and we work diligently to leverage the experiences and skill sets of our members. We hold ourselves to high standards of integrity, loyalty, and friendship when we are making business decisions.

Our forums meet quarterly, although individual members contact each other more frequently. For more information about The Investment Forum please visit us on the Web at www.vonzforum.com.

Kweisi Mfume was the guest of honor at the August 2006 forum. Pictured in the lower right is Michael Siebel, campaign finance manager, alongside Forum member Michael Bret Carr.

Here's to continued investment success

If I haven't convinced you yet that you need motivation along your investment journey, I'd like to share with you a message that I sent to my forum that provided many of them a renewed strength to go on. This message was equally empowering for me. Thanks again to all who attend the forums, and I look forward to providing you with many more forums in the future.

**Something to think about

   Growing up, my bus stop was about half a mile from my house. That was cool with me because I really didn't want the other kids to know where I lived. A few knew, but most of them didn't. Then one day most of them found out … oh boy, here we go. It was raining cats and dogs so the bus driver decided to take us right to our front doors. When the bus pulled in front of my house there was dead silence. I knew they were thinking, "I bet Von lives here." Unfortunately for me, they were right. They didn't say anything that day, but their facial expressions were enough. The comments came the next day. "You're poor!" "You live in a raggedy house!" "No wonder you have holes in your knees!" "That [those holes] didn't come from no playing marbles!"

   That's what they told me back then. Today the place where I live commands silence followed by very strong words, as well. However, it's a little different this time around. When you all enter my house to attend The Investment Forum, your responses of awe followed by very positive and inspirational statements make me appreciate the house I grew up in that much more. If I knew purchasing that house would have given so many people inspiration to feel charged and motivated before real estate or Wall Street were ever mentioned, I would have worked that much harder to do it sooner.

   I'm sure you didn't expect this type of follow-up story to how this weekend's forum turned out, but I would not have expected the level of motivation and passion for what we discussed would have been so strong, either. Some of the things that you all have shared leave me just as charged. I don't blame my parents for not having a finer place to raise me in. If someone had shared with them how to make investments in terms they could have understood then the chances of them living better would have been exponentially greater. That alone is enough to justify the existence of these forums. To me it's just a total waste to hoard information that you know can help someone else along. I don't understand why so many people play that game of tribal knowledge. There is plenty to go around. With that being said, for those of you who didn't have an opportunity to come, I need not say how the sharing of detailed financial information breeds an enormous amount of power and synergy.

   I sincerely hope these forums never disappoint any of you. It's a joy to see that so many people are interested in something I have to share. If I could just see the looks on the teachers' faces who put me in remedial classes in eighth grade when my Ukrainian class at Harvard told me, "When you talk, people want to listen. No seriously, it's like a gift." Perhaps it may silence them like it did those students on the bus. The funny thing is, I was speaking in French and Ukrainian. So if they got all that from a foreign language....

As I close, let me just set the record straight on my license plate, as apparently some people think I'm stuck up or conceited or whatever. The tag reads "2RCH4U." If the people who it annoys look just a little closer, there are five letters that precede it. Although only five letters, it is a name above all names, a name that has saved more fortunes than any investment advisor could ever advise, a name that even saves souls. The letters are J-E-S-U-S. So it's Jesus who is too rich for you, not me. I just consult Him and ask Him for things because the word around the campfire is He has the whole world in His hands. So if He's my Father and He's rich, shouldn't that make me rich, too? So please find something else to be annoyed by. The rest of us know the deal and need something of entertainment value when we're stuck in traffic. Just like "OBX" stands for Outer Banks, North Carolina.

Enjoy your summers. We'll do it again in a few months. Hey, Mike Jenkins, they should have never given you "people" money!

Anthony "Von" Mickle
—From the mobile home to where moguls roam
September 2007

About the Author

Take the talent from him and give it to the one who has the ten
talents. For everyone who has will be given more, and he will have
an abundance. Whoever does not have, even what he has will be
taken from him. And throw that worthless servant outside, into the
darkness, where there will be weeping and gnashing of teeth.
—Matthew 25:14

ANTHONY "VON" MICKLE is the president of The Investment Forum, a
real estate and equity investments group based out of the Washington
DC metropolitan area. He holds a Bachelor of Arts in modern languages
(French) and Bachelor of Science in business administration from The
Citadel, The Military College of South Carolina. He attended Harvard
University to study Ukrainian. He has an MBA from Keller Graduate
School and a certificate of financial planning from Georgetown
University. He is currently working on a Doctorate of International
Business from Breyer State University.

In his spare time, he enjoys spending time with his girlfriend
Crystal, four-wheeling on his estate, and flying helicopters. He regularly
returns to Camden, South Carolina, to visit his son Quandarius and
spend time with family.

Glossary

Abstract of title—A document used when determining if there are any previous claims on the property in question. The abstract is a written record of the property and helps to determine if the property can be transferred without any claims.

Adjustable-rate mortgage—A loan program where the interest rate may change at some point during the life of the loan. The terms of the adjustments are set when the loan is made.

Amortization—The time it takes for a loan to be fully paid off, with repayment in equal installments made at regular intervals.

Appraisal—A report that determines the current market value of a property. It is a must for any property you buy.

Broker—A specific industry professional who works to get you in touch with the product or service you require. You may have a mortgage or insurance broker, for example.

Cash out—Refinancing the loan on a mortgage to take cash out over the original amount of the loan.

Compound interest—Interest that accrues on the initial principal and the accumulated interest of a debt or principal deposit. Compounding allows a principal amount to grow at a faster rate than simple interest.

Credit report—A report that helps lenders decide how willing or able you are to repay your loan.

Credit score—A number between 300 and 850 that gives your report a rating on how well you have historically repaid your obligations. Investors should look to achieve and maintain a score of 700 or better.

Equity—The difference between what the property is worth and what you owe.

Escrow account—An account the mortgage company establishes to pay property tax and insurance during the term of the mortgage.

Foreclosure—What happens when the borrower continuously fails to make payments and the lender decides that the borrower is unwilling to make any significant attempts to save the property by setting up payment agreements.

Hazard insurance—Insurance that protects the property in the event of a natural disaster such as fire, wind, rain, or other various storms.

HELOC—Pronounced "he-lock," Home Equity Line of Credit. A loan taken against the value of the property when there is equity available. It works very similar to a home equity loan with the exception that you do not receive cash, but a line of credit instead.

Home inspection—A review of the property to check for structural damages and other defects that may require attention once the property is purchased.

Limited Liability Company (LLC)—A legal entity that limits the liability of its owners.

Market value—The property value at a specific time, which is represented by various items such as the local economy, interest rates, and consumer behavior.

Mortgage—A loan against the property.

Mortgage-backed securities—Securities that are traded on the open market that are backed by mortgages.

Multiple Listing Service (MLS)—A list of available properties that is made available to agents and brokers to show customers.

Positive cash flow—Making a profit after you have paid all monthly obligations on your investment property.

Principal balance—The amount you initially borrowed on a loan.

Probate—A hearing held that is used to transfer the assets of a deceased descendent to their legal heirs.

Refinance—Obtaining a new loan to replace the current one. In some cases, additional funds may be taken out over and above the original loan balance. See "Cash out."

S corporation—A legal business entity in which the income from the business is taxed only to its shareholders, which avoids a corporate-level tax.

Time value of money—The concept that a dollar today is worth more than a dollar in future years.

Underwriter—One who rates the acceptability of risks.

Index

www.ingramcontent.com/pod-product-compliance
Lightning Source LLC
Chambersburg PA
CBHW030800180526
45163CB00003B/1107